LAUGHTER AND THE LOVE OF FRIENDS

To Joanna Verney –
who has guided me through some of
the minefields of the publishing trade.

From quiet homes and small beginnings,
Out to undiscovered ends,
Nothing's worth the wear of winning,
But laughter and the love of friends.

Hilaire Belloc

Loving is what one has been through
with some one.

James Thurber

You lived in my life, I died in your
death. Those who can be parted, never loved.

Ronald Duncan in *Obsessed*

LAUGHTER AND THE LOVE OF FRIENDS
A MEMOIR 1945 TO THE PRESENT DAY

URSULA WYNDHAM

LENNARD PUBLISHING 1989

LENNARD PUBLISHING
a division of Lennard Books Ltd

Lennard House
92 Hastings Street
Luton, Beds LU1 5BH

British Library Cataloguing-in-Publication Data is available
for this title

ISBN 1 85291 061 5

First published in 1989
© Ursula Wyndham 1989

Phototypeset in Linotron Garamond by Input Typesetting
Ltd, London

Printed and bound in Great Britain by
Butler & Tanner Ltd, Frome and London

Cover design by Pocknell and Co.

Cover photographs of Petworth reproduced by permission
of The Royal Commission on the Historical Monuments of
England

CONTENTS

Foreword

*T*otal recall is not in nature. Memory is selective — and personal. No two witnesses see an occasion from the same angle. This, then, is an evocation of one woman's recollections and what she has learnt, and continues to learn, from life. Only the self-absorbed can suppose that growing old has no compensations. Ageing alters the emphasis on life, and the mutual reactions of individuals to each other, but these changes open up new areas of understanding and knowledge, in contacts with the present generation, which are infinitely rewarding in the light of what one has hitherto learnt in one's progress through this world, as one advances towards the next one.

In fiction both sides of the coin can be revealed. One of the drawbacks of real life is an insuperable inability to collect *all* the answers. In this story clues are dropped throughout the narrative. As, in hindsight, there is no devastating moment of realisation: merely the heightened awareness of recall, it is for the readers to make what deductions they choose.

Ursula Wyndham.
Petworth, 1988.

1

GETTING TO BE A GOATHERD

*M*y first remembered attempt at individuality was made at the age of twelve, when I asked permission of my mother to grow my hair, which had always been cut in a pudding basin bob, with a fringe, like any charity child. All fairy princesses had romantically long tresses like Rapunzel's, and it was well known that the crowning distinction of a woman's crowning glory was to have hair so long that she could sit on it. Perhaps, if I had hair that I could be seen to be able to sit on, somebody would notice me. The maternal answer was no, without any reason to back up the denial. No other mother's daughter had a charity child's head. After a long piteous wrangle, in which my mother strove to put an end to so tedious an argument as the hairstyle of a daughter whom, it appeared, she wished to keep as invisible as possible, I won the concession that I could grow it at the back and keep it plaited, while retaining the short crop over the ears.

This would certainly be eye-catching, especially in the early stages, but Rapunzel would probably never have needed her long tresses if she could only have used them to gain her heart's desire by leaning over backwards. It was the first of a life-time of compromises, and one of the least successful.

When I was thirteen years old my mother warned me of the onset of menstruation. Although I often met a female cousin, three years older than myself, my mother did not enquire if I was already aware of the information that she was about to hand out. Nor did I, in my turn, inform her that I had no need of her warning. Both parents, throughout my life with them, assumed in me a total lack of understanding of every aspect of sexual knowledge. I did not attempt to correct this hypothesis. In fact, in my thirties, when it appeared to me laughable, I took pains to encourage my father to make statements such as 'Ursula will not understand' when some faintly biological joke was being passed from mouth to mouth.

Nonetheless, the reiterated assumption, coupled with my father's frequently-stated complaints regarding my appearance — such as: 'Can *nothing* be done about that girl's spots?' To which my mother replied with a hasty 'Hush!' as though some irredeemable deformity had been mentioned, left me with the fixed impression that I was physically repulsive. Fortunately, in the circumstances, I was without sexual urges, although always deeply interested in the subject. In those days it was supposed that men only fell in love with attractive women. If a girl devoid of obvious physical charms none the less appeared to be popular with men, it was said that she was 'good in bed'. I did ponder how, ill-equipped as she was, she got into a position to prove her capabilities. Naturally, I did not ask my parents.

My non-relationship with them on all matters in which an exchange of views might have satisfied a deeply-felt need for reassurance, left me with a sense of a lack of identity, of character, of personality. I made the mistake of mentioning this implicit ignorance of how to address myself to any given situation as it arose. My mother, whose self-confidence had never been seen to waver, listened eyes averted, half bored, wholly uncomprehending. In the company of men I vaguely felt that some element of a feminine charm that I was positive I did not possess, was expected of me. With women the lack of personal identity was not important. 'I prefer my own sex, I think,' I told my mother. She gave a shriek. Once more I was silent. Why bother to attempt to protest that she had got me wrong yet again? Nearly twenty years had proved the ineffectuality of self-justification.

It was a Victorian concept, to which my parents adhered rigidly, that any show of love and affection was in the worst possible taste. No display of warmth of any kind had a place in their relationship with their children. My brothers and I were never kissed and cuddled. To kiss his sons would have spelt, for my father, a depraved act of perversion. Neither did we ever see our parents kiss or embrace each other. Yet their mutual devotion was subtly manifest. We were innately conscious of it. Conscious, too, that no such invisible flow of love passed between them and us. I think our situation would have been easier if we had not been conscious of this distinct love that our parents shared and we had no part in. It only served to muddle the issue. All signposts led to a dead end.

Conscious that I was the unwanted daughter in a family of three sons, and convinced that I carried every conceivable physical defect, I longed for a sister with whom to share confidences. The unfulfilled need for a confidante has dogged me throughout my life, leading to the assumption that, while as individuals we are not exactly predestined, we are born with, and carry along with us, certain acknowledged needs that we can either fight desperately to attain or to make it one of the lessons of our life to come to terms with doing without. In the first category comes the self-made man who, while naturally proud of his success with the odds stacked against him, will be hardened by the process and less sympathetic to weaker vessels. Similarly with regard to the frequent cry of parents that they want their children to have what they themselves never had. If they have never had it, why are they so sure that it, whatever that may be, is so desirable? We know what it is, in fact. Material possessions, combined with a higher style of living, in what is regarded as a superior neighbourhood. Bitter is the parental disappointment, resentful the filial lack of understanding, should the children of these people chance to secretly nurture freer dreams and wider aspirations. Or want no more than to take life as it comes.

The War offered release to many girls who were constricted

by parental rule at home. They learnt to perform a variety of jobs accurately and competently. It remains surprising how many reverted to the same parental rule when the War was over. They had received no training for any profession, nor had they received any encouragement to think for themselves. In fact that particular function was definitely discouraged. Mother or more likely father, always knew best.

Some young women had lost fiancés in the War, and cringed at the fear of inviting any further heartbreak. Apart from the reassuring knowledge that nobody was getting killed any more, the privations, that had obtained for five years, continued. The tedium of life increased: the shortage of food, petrol, clothes, the restrictions on travel, the lack of a settled existence — a future. Demobilisation was slow, so the normal contact between friends and relations which had been broken in 1939 was, in some cases, never resumed, if only because individual experiences had destroyed many of those mutual interests which are the essence of companionship. Peace was depressingly boring and uneventful. It bred two extremes: a restlessness that itched for new horizons, experiences, freedom from restrictions and taking orders. At the other end was the nesting instinct: to settle down, raise a family, cultivate a garden — and make that one's world's end. The women who failed in these aims were apt to withdraw completely into their local scenery or take to the bottle.

The aristocracy, by denuding itself of some portion of its vast possessions of lands, property and art treasures, for some time went on exactly as before. They had documentary evidence, covering a thousand years, to prove that they had survived invasions, crusades, conflicts, insurrections, plagues, poisonings, betrayals, attainders, arraignments, by not making a fuss about it at the time; by which means they husbanded what resources were left to them and handed down the invaluable qualities of knowing how to cope with events, and also with people on several different levels. Down the ages they had been accustomed to volunteer to serve their country or their king. The few who failed to do so earned the disapprobation of their peers.

Two episodes serve to sum up the prevailing atmosphere of

those years. Advantaged children had friends or relatives abroad who offered to shelter these innocents from the expected holocaust; others had not. The latter category were rallied to a sense of unity by the Queen. There was no question of the little princesses seeking safety in the Commonwealth. Queen Elizabeth announced: 'I cannot leave the King and my daughters cannot leave me.' The second episode concerns the popular move by Dr Edith Summerskill, Minister of Food in the post-war Labour government, taking sweets off the ration to appease a public hungry for self-cosseting. So great was the rush on these goodies that rationing had to be reintroduced.

I came home because, as far as I could see, nobody else wanted me. The first discovery I made was that my parents, too, came into that category. My eldest brother had been killed at El Alamein. It took no time to realise that my parents wished it had been me and that the constant reminder that this expendable offspring was still with them prevented the wound of my brother's death from healing. A cousin was told, to his face, by his mother, that she would have preferred his death to that of his elder brother. He admits hating her for it. I did not hate my father and mother for their equally obvious, though unspoken, sentiment. It was so much a part of what I had long grown accustomed to. What I now had to get used to, in the flat that we shared in Portman Square, was being invisible. It is an uncanny experience to be a ghost. Neither parent spoke to me, nor appeared conscious of my presence.

Since the War my father, too, had been without interests or occupations. He was becoming increasingly misanthropic. His day was divided between taking my dog, to whom he was uncommonly devoted, for a walk in Hyde Park, and reading. He read books on philosophy and theology, without discovering in them any harmony of thought or purpose. On Thursdays — the cook's day off — he lunched at the Turf Club.

My mother, by contrast, did not feel a need to seek any sort of elevating enlightenment. She knew exactly what she wanted and how to get it: interesting people to congregate round her dining room table and her card table. She read social memoirs and the novels of Maurice Baring and the author of *Elizabeth and her*

German Garden. Without great intelligence, she was extremely shrewd. She knew exactly how to promote conversation, by throwing an idea into the midst of the company and then drawing in the component members as though they were threads manipulated by one who works upon a loom. She had a strong family feeling of a kind I see little of nowadays. Before the War, when we lived in the country, she punctiliously asked her old aunts to stay, one by one, while my father was in London.

Now Sunday lunch was devoted to all her in-laws being gathered together as a weekly event. I heard her say once that a little Jewish blood was invaluable to inculcate business acumen into family veins. Lacking this advantage, she manifestly had a matriarchal streak. Because the wives of my father's two elder brothers were afflicted by bouts of, in the one case insanity, and increasing mental debility in the other, my mother's finger was foremost and firmly in every family pie. Jewish, too, was her instinct for doom and disaster: to be wailed over with a spirited despair of any redemption. A redeeming gleam would, indeed, have spoilt the whole act for her.

I never knew compassion in her. Yet once that grace had been hers. In 1921, her eldest sister-in-law had experienced her first bout of mental instability. It had been mooted that she should seek treatment in a psychiatric clinic in Freiburg. The journey had not, in the event, been made, but my mother had offered to go with her. The two sisters-in-law had never had anything in common. I pictured my mother in Freiburg with an unloved, mentally disturbed, relation by marriage: no Bridge, no dinner parties, no cronies, no gossip. 'Why,' I asked in amazement when, years later, I heard of this crisis, 'did you offer to go?'

'I felt sorry for her,' my mother replied, simply. I had never heard her utter those words before, nor was I to hear them again.

The drawing room, in the Portman Square flat, had double doors at one end, leading into the dining room. At the other end was the fireplace, with an armchair at either side and a sofa set back between the windows, at some distance from the hearth. When my brother John came back from Italy, in the train of Harold Macmillan, my mother ordered me to help her move an armchair into the drawing room from my father's study. I observed that there was room for my brother on the sofa where I sat. 'Don't be so stupid,' she said, 'it is too far from the fire.' After my brother's departure the chair was to be replaced whence it came. I spoke up, to ask that it might remain in the drawing room, since I, too, would be grateful for the warmth from the fire. My mother looked intensely annoyed, but made no comment. She did, however, move her own chair more towards the centre of the hearth, so that there was no room for what was now my chair in the cosy fireside circle. On cold evenings I requested room to insert my chair. My mother, in irritated tones, muttered: 'Very well, push me to one side.' I exerted my strength to shove her and her chair back to its usual position near the wall. She would almost immediately cry: 'Not *this* far!' so that the circle round the fire became anything but cosy.

I enjoyed just one rather notable privilege, which I found surprising, since it was totally at variance with my otherwise constant role of non-existence. Before the War we had lived in a house in Cadogan Square. It was sold, but my parents retained the mews flat and garage at the back. In this reposed the small car that my mother had used for short journeys during the War. This car was kept licenced and insured for my personal use. It was a tremendous boon.

One morning my mother broke her habitual silence to enquire, in casual tones, whether I would care to go and live in the garage flat. I am sure she had never seen this apartment. It had no central heating and the bath stood in one corner of the dusty concreted garage; reached, from the flat above, by a ladder-like staircase. If I had to be miserable, I at least recognised the advantage of being miserable in comfort. I uttered an astonished no; hoping that a discussion of alternatives might ensue. My mother merely looked annoyed and the state of non-communication returned. I did not, myself, take the initiative as I was never listened to, which increased my sense of isolation and peculiar ghostliness.

I took a typing course, at which I proved to be somewhat inept, and then worked, voluntarily, for the Soldiers, Sailors' and

Airmens' Families Association. Because I could use a typewriter and string words together I was put to answering the correspondence. I was not entirely successful at this, since I answered each letter individually and not according to the set rules laid down, with which I was all too familiar in my own life. Every problem, whether written or expressed by an individual in person who came to seek help, was dealt with by rote. No personal interest had any place in the conduct of affairs. I gave up this work, since it made me feel as powerless to help others as I was to help myself. From then on I lost hope. I saw no plan, no future, no point in my life. I did not feel like taking it, since I feared total oblivion more, being already exceedingly close to it. My whole bodily metabolism slowed down and I virtually ceased to menstruate.

The crunch came under incredible circumstances. My parents were accustomed to go on a round of visits in August, while the servants had their annual holiday. I was informed of the dates of their departure and return. For that period, I, too, must be away from home. Where, it concerned them not. For the August of 1948 I had been unable to make my plans tally exactly with theirs. I would not be departing till two days after them.

'That is impossible,' stated my mother. 'You cannot stay here.'

'Why not?' I asked.

'Don't be stupid, you know perfectly well that you cannot stay alone in the flat.'

I had to pinch myself to recollect that I was the same woman who had been offered the rest of her life alone in the derelict garage flat.

'Why can't I stay here alone for just two days?'

'Don't be such a bore. There will be nobody to cook for you.'

'I can do everything necessary for myself.'

My mother said that she was tired of the argument. The idea was too ludicrous to be thought of. I think I must have had what the French call a *crise de nerfs*. I cannot remember anything of the ensuing few minutes. My next recollection is of going to the telephone in the pantry and ringing up the Angel Hotel at Midhurst, which civilly agreed to shelter me and my dog Sancho for two nights.

Later still, my mother announced, with the patience of an angel, that, at great trouble, she had obtained the services of a woman to come in and do for me during the disputed two days. I had the pleasure of telling her, with cold dignity — after all, I was my mother's daughter — that I had made other plans and would not need the flat. I refused to divulge my destination, in which interest had never previously been shown.

From Midhurst I went for long walks with my dog and meditated on my situation. To this day, when I drive to Midhurst, I turn my eyes towards the triangle of land, bordered by the two drives to Cowdray House and the main road that runs through the park. On that patch of grass I lay on my back, gazing up at a cloudless sky, and tried in earnest to devise a means of struggling through the clouds that choked my existence. My entire income was derived from a settlement that brought in £300 a year. Half of this sum my father retained to pay for my keep. I knew nothing of finance, nor how to borrow money, but if only I could find a barn to live in, I would subsist on weeds and berries rather than continue the shameful solitude of being a pensioner under my father's inhospitable roof.

When I got back to London I left my name on the books of one or two house agents and scanned the advertisements dealing with house property; but the hope was still far short of reality. I said nothing to my parents on the subejct that occupied all my thoughts. About two months after that fateful August I was summoned into my father's presence to be informed of a decision he and my mother had made, as usual without any discussion with the person it concerned. He had arranged to break the terms of my brother, Henry's, will, which had bequeathed his money, in turn, to his two younger brothers, so that a capital sum be made available to purchase a small cottage. A further sum would form a heavily controlled trust fund, the income of which would produce between £500 and £600 a year.

By a stroke of the pen I, who a couple of months earlier had been deemed incapable of fending for myself for two nights, was now to be cast upon the world as a householder on an income which both parents would have considered as totally insufficient to support life. My mother's ear, so close to the ground in all social affairs, heard that Lord Haig was selling his cottage in the village of Sutton, near Pulborough, in West Sussex. On a day of pouring rain in November I took the train to Pulborough and a taxi to Sutton, to inspect Rose Cottage. It was an unpretentious two-bedroomed building of flint-stone with red brick quoins and window surrounds. It stood in its own orchard, with the well that had supplied its water, still in place, but filled in, standing beyond the back door.

The next question to be solved was what to do with each day while living alone in the country. Gardening and housekeeping I regarded as chores. I needed an interest and a responsibility. An instant answer came into my mind out of the air: keep goats. This was puzzling and out of context, as I had never met a goat, knew nothing whatever about them, nor how to milk them. Yet the impression that my future life was to be in the guise of a goatherd persisted. The immediate difficulties were solved by the positive action of a normally most unpositive friend. She told me that her aunt in Devon kept goats and that she would immediately get in touch with this unfortunate woman and tell her to expect me for a week's stay to learn all there was to know about goat-keeping. I ventured to suggest that this arbitrary plan might not suit the aunt, but was told she was one of those who coped with things.

She certainly was. Her name was Joyce Carew. She and her husband were both Devonians. She had a keen appetite for salacious gossip which, through contact with my mother's friends, I was able to give her. She was much intrigued by my imminent emergence into rural life and bore me off to a meeting of the local Women's Institute. I felt a fool singing 'Jerusalem' and was told later, that after that I fell asleep.

Perhaps I may have been a goat in a previous incarnation; I felt such an affinity with them. Intelligent, affectionte, obstinate, they appeared to be forever on the alert to gauge what was expected of them and then to do the opposite. They had the human charac-teristic of being certain that the grass must be greener on the opposite side of the fence, coupled with the most inhuman power of getting under, through or over every obstacle.

2

FRIENDS ON THE ROAD

M y parents were so frightened that I would find life alone in the country beyond my control and that I would wander, waif-like, back into their midst, that they gave up the lease of the flat in Portman Square, which had two spare bedrooms, and moved to one in Hereford House, near Marble Arch, that had none, They thus cut off their noses to spite their faces, since this unnecessary precaution made them equally unable to offer hospitality to their sons, a circumstance that increased my father's sense of isolation and boredom and misanthropy.

I was thus able to retain my bedroom furniture. I bought a second-hand suite of a sofa and two armchairs and picked up an elegant Regency-style writing table for £13 in a shop in Baker Street. My mother, on an imprudent impulse, had bought six lyre-back chairs, which must have been knocked together by some enthusiastic amateur backroom boy, since they were apt to suddenly disintegrate under the weight of the human body. My mother's plan to use them as dining room chairs in place of the large stately ones she and my father had started their married life with, led to marked apprehension among her guests and I got the four remaining ones. I still have one survivor, which I use as a bedroom chair. I bought a flawed dining table very cheaply. My brother John and his wife made me a generous present of kitchen equipment, crockery was cheap; so, with these basic requirements, I moved into Rose Cottage, Sutton, in March 1949. Shortly afterwards I took delivery of two goats that arrived, through the agency of Joyce Carew, from Devon.

A previous owner, who had carried out the modernisation of the house, informed me where I could obtain the title deeds. These went back to the year 1720 and proved that prior to the modernisation, Rose Cottage had been known, for over two hundred years, as Brown's House. Rose Cottage is a boring name, since nearly every village has one. I changed the name of my new home back into Brown's possession. Sometimes I felt I shared the house with him. I reckoned he must have been something of a loner too. A man who lived by his principles, minded his business and was something of a personality in his day, so that passers-by said to each other: 'Aye, that's Brown's house, that is.'

For some time it seemed nothing less than a miracle to be able to say to myself that the house, the garden, the goats, all my cheap but immensely precious possessions, belonged to me, who had hitherto never considered the possibility of having anything to call my own. Things to be shared by anybody in need, with anybody who was friendly and congenial and on my wavelength. In the book of Irish fairy tales that I had read as a child I had been enchanted by the recorded notion that the Land of Faery is entered unknowingly. Superficially it looks like the landscape that you are accustomed to. You come to realise that you have entered into that magic land only as you notice that the grass is greener, the flowers brighter, the sky bluer, the sunshine more golden and dreams are fact. I had stepped through the invisible barrier.

Not for long, naturally. 'The world is too much with us, late and soon.' I had an old Ford van, whose battery made a habit of ceasing to operate at moments of great necessity. The cottage water supply was heated by a boiler which did not care for coke. Anthracite, which was the boiler's favourite food, was in short supply and could only be obtained occasionally. Too many hours of several days a week were spent lighting and relighting again and again this recalcitrant heater.

The nearest person in need was a widowed Mrs Penfold, who lived next door. It was virtually impossible to step out of the back door without Mrs Penfold's head appearing above the dividing fence and Mrs Penfold's voice uttering a string of platitudes and questions. It was no escape to return indoors and shut the back door. Within minutes Mrs Penfold came knocking at it, bearing gifts of tarts, scones or cakes, baked unappetisingly by Mrs Penfold's heavy hand.

Her life was certainly not one to be envied. Having lost the seemingly unlamented Mr Penfold, he had been, all too soon, replaced by her elderly bachelor brother, in poor health, who looked to his sister to wait on him hand and foot. On one occasion she asked me to take her brother into Petworth with me. He would then, later, catch the bus home. At the same time she handed me a broken clock, with a request to take it to the repairer. I accepted the second commission somewhat coldly, thinking why on earth could not the brother perform this task? I was glad that I had kept this thought to myself, as Mrs Penfold's brother proceeded to have a heart attack in Petworth, mercifully not in my presence, and was returned to poor Mrs Penfold, all too soon, in a taxi.

Another neighbour in Sutton, much more valuable in my need to learn ease of communication with people, was Deirdre Balfour, the beautiful and charming sister of Rupert Hart Davis. She and her teenage daughter, Annabel, who took an interest in my goats, were joyful company. Deirdre was endearingly open about her fears and weaknesses. Neurosis was, to her, an old friend whom she would not have known how to get on without.

She lent me a book called *Be Glad You're Neurotic*, by an American called Dr Bisch. Dr Bisch took a depressing view of human sanity, or the lack of it. At the end of the book he set out a test in the form of questions. To be considered normal it was necessary to score 85% of the answers right. Dr Bisch's idea of right, that is. Anybody scoring less than 70% was definitely in need of help. I was astonished to score 80%. After reading this work my reaction was that should I be in America, on the verge of a nervous breakdown, my last coherent words would be: 'Keep me out of Dr Bisch's hands!'

Deirdre's books were all of a cheer-yourself-up variety. I found the incentive they meant to induce a turn-off in itself. A book enumerating various Delights, collected by J. B. Priestley, alienated me by including 'playing with children' among the number. At the same time I was filled with a grudging admiration that people like Priestley and Rose Macauley could find so much to be delighted about, and could go on about these passing pleasures for a whole chapter. I had to admit that the chapter on Grumbling was a good read. The reflection that the only two things that I could call to mind that gave me recurrent pleasure were lying in the bath and going to bed, led to the deduction that I might as well be dead. I could have added that the society of such as Deirdre Balfour gave me a lot of pleasure. One of Deirdre's books, James Thurber's *Leave Your Mind Alone*, I found hilarious.

That Deirdre had a more serious taste in literature I found when Annabel informed me that she and her mother and Deirdre's second husband, a handsome barrister called Tony Bland, whom she had recently married, had been lent Graham Greene's villa at Capri. No rent was demanded, but each of them was to leave a book behind when they left. 'I've a good mind to leave an Amelianne story,' threatened Annabel, darkly. Tony Bland had fixed on *Flaubert and Madame Bovary*, on which subject I am sure Dr Bisch would have plenty to say. Deirdre was not leaving *Be Glad You're Neurotic*, which might have rung a bell with Graham Greene, but, instead, a biography of Florence Nightingale.

At Bignor, the next village up the road, lived Mr and Mrs Hill, parents of Heywood Hill, the bookseller. Mrs Hill spoke in a quavering voice, as though about to burst into tears, but had in fact a character that made an act of pleasure out of very little material. During Goodwood week, at the end of July, she was wont to take sandwiches, walk about three miles (she must have been at least seventy years old), to the Chichester road and sit there, eating her sandwiches and watching the Goodwood traffic rumble up Duncton Hill. Her eyes sparkled as she spoke of it. Mr

Hill, a quiet man, always referred to his wife as 'her' and 'she'; yet I felt that there was a close bond between them. I did wonder whether, earlier in their married life, she had fought a losing battle to be taken to Goodwood Races, rather than watching other people go to them.

At Bignor Park lived Lord and Lady Mersey. Lady Mersey was the sister of my mother's old friend, Horatia Seymour. Both she and her husband were very kind to me. Lord Mersey was a law unto himself. His wife had given up trying to exert a restraining influence over him. His sons seldom spoke in his presence. He enjoyed relating an endless repertoire of stories, not all in the best of taste. Some he narrated in French, although they would have been no less pungent in English. Lord Mersey's friend, Sir Harry Luke, caught this habit. Once, when I was lunching with the Merseys, Sir Harry told a story, of inordinate length, in strongly English-accented French. He then condescendingly repeated it, in English, for my benefit. Lord Mersey sat with Buddha-like impassivity during Sir Harry Luke's performance. When, at length, it was over, he told a story of his own, in his excellent French, looking at me as he told it, and not adding a translation. I kept my eyes, beadily, on Sir Harry Luke.

I can only recollect one aphorism from Lord Mersey's rich vein of anecdote:

> If a diplomat says yes, he means maybe. If he says maybe, he means no. If he says no, he's no diplomat.
> If a lady says no, she means maybe. If she says maybe, she means yes. If she says yes, she's no lady.

Lord Mersey saw no reason, either, not to be embarrassing in his own house. At his lunch table he asked me, on one occasion, if I knew Mrs Hart? At the same time that I said that I did not; who was she? Lady Mersey moaned: 'Oh Clive, not *again*!' As if she had not spoken, Lord Mersey continued on the subject of Mrs Hart. 'Well, she lives in east Sussex, she has eleven gardeners, and she smells *simply* delicious — all over!' Unfortunately I thought this funny and had the greatest difficulty in not laughing.

Lord Mersey was also an embarrassment to me on the Sundays

when Holy Communion was celebrated. He and I were not sacra-
mentalists. Lady Mersey was. As they came to church by car, he
had to wait for her until the service was over. To pass the time he
ensured that I waited with him. It became his habit to lead me
behind a tombstone and begin his story-telling. I felt that I was
being forced into a rather undignified role, while lacking the
courage and savoir faire to avoid it. Instead I found myself giggling,
which increased my sense of an unbecoming situation and also
attracted attention.

Lord Mersey was utterly impervious to the opinions of others.
Had he felt the impulse, he would have danced naked on the
graves. In one of these churchyard encounters he cheerfully told
Mrs Hill that she must be sexually deranged, because she admitted
having enjoyed the performance of a popular actor in a current
film. Sometimes his stories, on these occasions, were biographical,
as when he told me of the Ladies Mary and Isabel Brown, daughters of Lord Sligo ('before your time'), of one of whom it had
been written (probably by Lord Mersey):

I thought I saw a butter-pat
Upon the Sussex down.
I looked again and saw it was
The Lady Mary Brown.
And are you standing up? I said,
Or are you sitting down?

'Everyone said,' Lord Mersey informed me, 'that Lady Isabel was
the one to marry.'

'How could they tell?' I wanted to know, 'I fear Lady Isabel
can't have been virtuous.'

'I can promise you she couldn't have been anything else,'
stated Lord Mersey, uncompromisingly, 'but she never did marry,
because people realised that if you married Isabel, you got Mary
as well.'

I looked them up. Their father, the second Marquess of Sligo,
was even more unfortunate than mine. He married three times.
His two first wives each had a single female child, who died young.

His third wife, a French woman, produced twin daughters, who were christened Mary Isabel and Isabel Mary respectively.

After Lord Mersey died, the Times published a biographical obituary, proving that there was no corner of the globe into which Lord Mersey had not penetrated, no adventure that he had not master-minded, no experience known to man, that he had not encountered. I was told that Lord Mersey had written it himself.

I spent a lot of time herding my goats by the roadside, so that they could browse on the hedgerow and eat the grass on the verges. To pass the time, while they were so engaged, I took the opportunity to read the whole of the Old Testament. The two clearest recollections I retain are the heartbreaking description of despair, so emotively described in the story of David and Absalom, and the pure pornography of the Song of Solomon, made all the more profane by claiming to be a picture of the Church. Nobody notices or comments on this anomaly. I was sufficiently impressed to commit to memory suitable sections and produce them, some years later, as my own opinion during pillow-talk. I can vouch for their effectiveness.

Foot passengers stopped for a word. I remember asking the roadman if he had had a good holiday? He replied yes, but he had had back luck since. Asked what sort of bad luck? Mr Francis answered, in the same tone of voice, 'My wife died on Sunday.' I had yet to learn how to cope with any revelation concerning human suffering and was considerably embarrassed and taken aback. These apprehensions proved, as they should be, unnecessary. In the present instance Mr Francis explained that he was looking forward to going to live with his married daughter in Portsmouth. He said he liked Portsmouth better than Sutton. But Mrs Francis would never consider such a move.

On another occasion Tony Bland came striding along exercising the Balfour poodles. I thought him nice, but rather austere, and was a little frightened of him. I decided to do no more than pass the time of day with him, in case I cut a poor figure and made some idiotic remark through shyness. However, he stopped, remarked upon the weather and said that Deirdre had a cold. I ventured to ask how they had enjoyed Capri? He said it had been lovely, with perfect weather and a lot of interesting queer folk, like Norman Douglas, who had been joined by Somerset Maugham. The latter announced that he was revisiting all the places where he had been happy, before he died. I exclaimed that that sounded a most depressing pastime, with which Tony agreed. He added that he had ceased to be a barrister: it was such hard work. He was now a don, lecturing on Law at London University.

The wife of one of Lord Mersey's woodmen was a regular passenger on the road between Bignor and Sutton. She told me that she had been one of thirteen children, but had only two of her own. 'I had a girl and then I had a boy. I said to my husband: "There you are, there's one of each. There aren't any other sorts I can give you, so I am packing it in." '

Country characters had not yet died out in the 1950s. There was Mr Knight, who worked at the gas works in Petworth and was famed for a certain individuality of self-expression. When his family begged him to buy a bicycle to save the long walk to work, he replied that it was not necessary. He could get there just as quickly on his feet, even if it did take him a little longer. Unable to find his cap, he requested his wife's help in searching for it. She pointed out that it was on his head. Mr Knight was properly grateful. 'Thank goodness you told me, else I would have gone off without it!'

Another character was the road mender's sister, Daisy Francis. She had a smallholding of about half a dozen cows. She, too, sometimes herded them beside the road, where I chatted to her. She lived alone and had no regular assistance. She must have worked incredibly hard. It left her with no time to wonder whether she was happy or not, nor whether she would have done better to have steered her life along a different course. We agreed that if you keep animals whose welfare and health takes precedence of your own, considerations like housekeeping and cleaning, tidy clothes and appearance, come a poor second and are dealt with as and when. Daisy had a healthy contempt for those vapid mortals who had nothing better to think of than their looks and the latest fashions. She was full of folk lore, herbal remedies and the effects of the waxing and waning of the moon. In another era Daisy would have been designated a white witch. In another era I might have been her acolyte.

Daisy's cottage was outside the village. Mine stood right in the middle of it. My goats followed me like dogs, but to walk down the village street with them loose meant that they would nip through any garden gate and ravage the flowers. I had the village blacksmith make me three chains linked at one end, with a longer chain as a lead. I drove three of the goats, thus tied together, before me to a grazing area beyond the village and led the fourth goat with my other hand. I am a child of nature. The sunshine on my bare skin is a delight, to enjoy which I possessed the 1950s version of the bikini. I debated long as to whether Sutton was ready for this garment and finally, ravished by the golden days, stepped out to go goat-herding thus lightly clad and feeling distinctly self-conscious.

Sutton took not the slightest notice. Or so I thought. In 1988 an elderly man approached me in Petworth and, with a wicked look in his eye, informed me that he had never forgotten my daily progress through Sutton, wearing a bikini.

I was very lucky to begin my personal life in an unspoilt country village of the kind that is no longer known in the commuter belt of the home counties. Everybody knew and was on equal terms with everybody else. Besides the blacksmith's forge there was a village shop which took an interest in stocking the commodities that individuals wanted. Mr Harland, the owner, was reputed to be a socialist, a rare animal in that neck of the woods, but having no audience he did not make a thing about it, although he was always definite in his views on any subject. One need not fear to ask a favour of him. Plagued by rats in my corn store, I set a trap. It caught a fine adult specimen. How does one execute a captive rat? Not by drowning. I had tried letting an unwanted kid drop from its mother's womb into a bucket of water. Although it can have hardly breathed, it was several minutes before it ceased its struggles to survive. I could not face that ordeal again. Instead I confidently set out with the rat in the trap, to the village shop to ask Mr Harland to do the fell job for me. The rat knew exactly the object of the journey. Its little human-like hands gripped the bars of the trap and it shrieked the whole way, in mortal dread.

When I was ten years old I had watched a man skinning a dead horse at the fox-hound kennels in Petworth Park. I had asked him how he could bring himself to perform such a task. He replied: 'Some one has to.' It made a strong impression on me. If a job needs to be done, what right has anybody to back off from it? I could not kill that rat because I did not know how to. I never set another trap.

I took the breeding of goats very seriously; studying the herd books and driving the individual females long distances in the van to the males whose blood lines, I reckoned, would unite with theirs to produce perfect kids. In spite of these efforts I never bred a champion. I sold cream to a local restaurant and, before meat was derationed, sold unwanted kids for food. This was a difficult decision. Baby kids are the most attractive of all young animals. But as I could not keep them all and they would have to be put down anyway, it seemed only sensible to make useful money out of the sorry business. Keeping any livestock hardens one. I became, perforce, a capable goat midwife, although it was a task I always disliked. It took me back to the rigours of my VAD days. Goats, impervious to pain if flogged for a misdemeanour, scream like women when giving birth.

My mother, when I told her this, said that it reminded her of Lady Winchelsea, who had yelled so loud when in labour in her own home, that frantic neighbours had battered on the door, thinking somebody was being murdered. It had been Lord Winchelsea's awkward duty to face the mob, with the news that the howls were only due to his wife in the natural course of giving birth.

My mother, astonished to discover that I was capable of making social contact with the kind of people she considered worth knowing, was now keeping in regular contact with me, by telephone. She would have made an excellent professional gossip columnist, with her insatiable determination to keep in touch with every aspect of human drama and folly. Always a sound sleeper, she woke, alert, at eight o'clock each morning. Oblivious of the possibility that some of her friends might not have gone to bed until dawn, she hastened to reach for the telephone and begin a long list of calls, opening with the words: 'What's the news?'

At eight o'clock in the morning I was milking my goats. They lived, in confined quarters, in one half of the coal shed. They were milked in the kitchen. I sat, they stood, on a low wooden platform. If I left one, while I answered the telephone, it rampaged all over the house or, if I shut the kitchen door, broke everything within sight. I explained to my mother that 8 a.m. was not an hour at which I was free to tell her the news. I was not particularly surprised that she took not the slightest notice of my request to make her calls to me at a later hour. I did not subsequently reply if the telephone rang before 9 a.m.

When my mother rang again, later in the day and I reminded her that eight o'clock was a fruitless time to ring me, she indignantly denied having made the earlier call. Nobody else ever tried to contact me at that hour. Her denial confirmed something so upsetting that I had hitherto refused to acknowledge it to myself, namely that my mother was a shameless liar. By contrast my father was brutally literal. Inheriting with his genes his belief that truth is very important in the conduct of one's life and the pathway of one's thoughts, I had, at the same time, learnt from his uncaring capacity to hurt, to temper this dangerous weapon in consideration of other people's feelings.

The final acceptance that my mother was on no account to be trusted, possibly played its part in my inability to forget my past experiences at their hands and to relive, in their presence, every feeling of inadequacy, unattractiveness, stupidity, even when they were being perfectly civil. I have never entirely succeeded in coming to terms with this vulnerability. I have, however, noticed that those who exploit it are invariably in a like situation of failing to accept some psychological weakness in themselves.

3

CAN *THIS* BE LOVE?

*T*his then was the village life of which I was now a part, connected with my old life only by my mother's telephone calls. Beyond the village there was the hunting and racing scene. My father kept a horse at livery in the Chiddingfold and Leconfield Hunt country. This animal became more and more at my disposal as my father found that, with the other aspects of his life, this which was once his greatest pleasure, was losing its power to please. He complained that his hunter was becoming too frolicsome for him when suggesting, with increasing frequency, that I should ride it instead. It was, in fact, an extremely stolid animal, fit to pull the Lord Mayor's coach, between whose traces it would not have looked out of place.

The cheerful people I met in the hunting field also assembled at Fontwell Park Racecourse. I never took to racing, although it was my fate, in the years to come, to spend a lot of time at race meetings; but Fontwell was a small friendly meeting, where one was sure to meet people one knew and would not otherwise come into contact with. Also, there was the occasional insane element that lent an aura of make-believe to the scene.

At one meeting a cheerful, irresponsible girl, well known in the district, thought that it would be a lark to start the bidding for a selling plater that was being sold in the paddock after a race. She opened the bidding at £50, confident that others would take it up. Nobody did. The horse was hers. Her poignant cries attracted the foxhunters: the field-master, the vet, a trainer friend of the field-masters, myself and other race-goers. We went, in a body, to inspect the horse in its box. The vet examined its legs and announced not one of them to be sound. It was a miracle that it had completed the course, let alone won. The field-master and the trainer went into a huddle, then hurried off to interview the owner. He agreed to take the horse back into his possession in exchange for the day's expenses. In the last race was a 20 to 1 outsider called No Bid. It seemed an omen. One should never ignore them. I put £1 on it. It won!

So 1949 turned into 1950. On the 1st of January I recorded in my diary:

> Couldn't get to sleep last night and the church bell began to toll at midnight, which was somehow unutterably depressing. One felt one's life was racing by and in about 5 minutes one would be old and dead. This morning all the papers harping on the 'turn of the century' note, which produced same feelings.

It was in the hunting field that I first became aware that the impression left by my parents that I was physically unattractive and bereft of feminine charm was not shared by other people. Within a year of my freedom I found myself being propositioned. I have never had any pretensions, never yearned for the might-have-been. Life is complicated enough as it is. I was quite content to be a virgin. It was an unlooked for relief to be wanted — and by a not unattractive man, who looked well on a horse; but barring the reassurance that I was, after all, desirable, I wanted none of it. And said so. The information not only had no effect, it seemed to act as an incentive. So be it. I knew exactly what to do. To pay no attention. Pretend it wasn't happening. Slip out of range like an eel. Why is nothing in life as simple as it ought to be? I disliked being kissed. I disliked being touched. Still disliking any form of contact, I yet found I missed it, and him, when he was no longer present. This was frightening. I was not, as I had supposed, in control of the situation. Instincts that I had been certain that I did not possess, were taking control of me.

It was a challenge and I fought it, doggedly, for months, nine in all. I deduced that my opponent had not only had considerable experience with women, but, what is much rarer, an intimate understanding of their feelings. While I rigidly suppressed mine, he expressed them, accurately, for me. 'I took you by surprise.' 'You are nervous.' 'I am sorry I frightened you.' 'I won't do anything that you don't want.' 'You have nothing to fear.' 'Just tell me when you are ready.' Everything that I was denying to myself was expressed by him. It cut the grass from under my feet. It removed my defences as soon as I set them up. It was very unfair. Worse than unfair, the whole concept was becoming, against my will, fascinating. Not so much William himself, as what he stood for in the area of my rising self-awareness. Just at the right moment he intruded the information that he loved me. It was a much too disturbing possibility to add to the general turmoil. I did not believe it. To the orderly Virgo character it was, at the same time, what should be, and a disreputable complication, in view of the fact that he had a strong-minded wife in the background, with whom I was on good terms.

I recalled, with thankfulness, the words of Smollett's heroine in *Humphrey Clinker*. When asked why she had no inclination to marry the eminently suitable choice of a husband that her father had made for her, she replied that while the man in question undoubtedly possessed every quality to make most women happy, yet, for her, he lacked 'that nameless charm that captivates and controls the enchanted spirit.' I was indeed controlled, but not, thank God, captivated.

What is the basis of that nameless charm that not every woman needs? As a Virgo whose passions, unless aroused, were entirely dormant, I recognised the danger of allowing an involvement to which my whole heart did not respond and that failed to evoke a wider understanding of love as an emotion that should heighten our awareness, not only of the needs of our fellow creatures, but also of a broader appreciation of nature and life in the fullest sense.

I was intrigued by several aspects of William. There was his quiet and graceful mastery of horses, his understanding of the human spirit in general and the fears and foibles of women in particular; his eyes: intelligently expressive and interrogatory. Lightly fascinated by his interest in me, I yet did not feel sufficiently involved to question its cause or motivation. More likely I feared, instinctively, whatever would loosen my control over my own emotions.

The fret and fear and loneliness of indecision were bridged by the blissful comradeship of conversation. Cerebrally we had little in common. I once asked him what he knew of Richard III, having read Josephine Tey's book, *Daughter of Time*, and considered that all her characters' minutely precise knowledge of that monarch's much disputed personality were far from true in real life. My would-be lover's confident assertion: 'You mean the horse? He's a five-year-old stallion,' was the most positive answer I got, having put the question to several people. My laughter offended his pride. On the subject of the peccadilloes and peculiarities of our mutual friends we discoursed for hours. His knowledge of human nature cast an interesting and discussable light on such debates.

We were now well into 1951. As soon as some rationing was discontinued tremendous plans for the celebration of the centenary of the Great Exhibition began to be discussed, to the alarm of all the more cautious elements of the population. In view of the poverty of the country and the dismal state of the world, to embark on elaborate plans for a glorious Festival of Britain appeared to be a pathetic mockery. Mr Herbert Morrison stated the case in favour rather well.

> To organise the Festival of Britain now may be madness, but it is the sort of madness that has got us on the map and is going to keep us there . . . I hope that our courage and faith in holding this Festival — the first time in history that a whole great nation has put itself on display — will give this distracted world a message as full of meaning in its way as the message that went round the world from Dunkirk.

The Festival covered a broader area of interests than perhaps many people suspected. The *Daily Telegraph* carried a headline: No Fleas For Festival. Circus Plan Held Up By Shortage.

> The Festival of Britain is not likely to be able to stage a flea circus at Battersea Park. The promotors' advertisements have drawn blank. This is said to be due to a shortage of fleas. Mr Billy Rayner, the owner of the flea circus, who would have taken the contract if he could, has advertised for them without success. The fleas, he explained, must come from human beings; fleas from animals die when they leave the animal. 'If only I could get twelve fleas within the next week,' he said, 'I could open at Mitcham Common at Easter, but I must have a certain amount of time to train them. Since the war the flea situation has been getting steadily worse. I blame the vacuum cleaners and new-fangled disinfectants. The average flea lives only for about three months, and they do not breed in captivity. Towards the end of three months they become stiff-jointed, just like humans in their old age. And then they cannot ride the cycles, pull chariots or do sword fighting. All the old fleas can manage is the occasional dance. The public won't pay to see that. It is just what they expect from fleas anyway. We usually find that the more educated people are, the more interest they take in our fleas. At Oxford we bring the house down.' Mr Rayner said that the North, particularly Newcastle-on-Tyne, had always been their best source of fleas. They proposed to advertise in the local press.

I did not attend any of the Festival events. My duties as a goat keeper kept me at home, as did my limited income, but I began to feel a need to broaden my interests and horizons. Joyce Carew and her husband were planning to rent a villa near Grasse, in the South of France for the opening months of 1952. She suggested I should either stay with them in Devon before they left England or be a paying guest at the villa. I opted for the latter and was saving towards the scheme.

The sexual siege ended around the end of the year. Apart from all the other very disturbing factors involved, which were so disruptive to the routine of daily life and a wider range of thought, I had decided that, upon the whole, it would be a pity to die wondering. Suppose if, in my fifties, I was left with the realisation that I had let slip the opportunity for one natural experience that, even prior to its fulfilment, had such a profound effect upon my sensibilities — and that now it was too late; bitterness, combined with a latent fear of any adventure, such as I notice in so many older women, widowed or single, would be the only emotion left to me. It seemed safer not to risk that cul de sac.

In fact, the through road proved nothing short of petrifying. While awaiting my would-be lover I was suddenly seized by a stark animal terror, amounting to a fear of murder, which proved so impossible to rationalise that I locked both the front and back doors and went to ground, as it were, refusing to answer the doorbell or to give any indication of my presence in the house. It was not until after he had been and gone that I came to myself to any degree. The terror abated and was succeeded by a sense of shame at how inhumanly I had been forced, by inexplicable insensate fear of what I had thought that I wanted, to behave.

Psychologists would have a field day finding intricate family reasons for my overwhelming dread. It is not unknown in the animal kingdom, where escape is seldom possible. Some of my goatlings shivered with horror on being presented to the male goat, made every effort to escape from their halters, and had to be forcibly restrained to accept an act that takes, in the case of a goat, no more than a minute. My contrite apologies and pleas for forgiveness were met, as usual, by an understanding: 'You were frightened, weren't you?' A tolerance that took into account the fact that he had virtually won the day.

At the end of January, 1952 I left my goats at a goat farm near Worthing and my dog and cat at the vet's kennels and set off for the south of France. With me went a friend, Joan Alexander, whose fiancé had been killed in Korea. After the shock of the news, she had given up her job and returned to her parents, where she had been vegetating for a year and was beginning to understand that lack of occupation does nothing to help acceptance of bereavement. We travelled by train to Paris, where we stayed two nights. Food rationing was still operating in England and the standard and the amount of food waiting to be consumed on the train between Calais and Paris was equal to a banquet. We over-ate considerably.

A friend of my mother's had recommended the Hotel France et Choiseul, in the Rue St Honore, as being comfortable and moderate in price. It was doubtless the moderate price that was responsible for the fact that our comfortable bedroom on the first floor had no private bath, and that the only public bath in the entire hotel was situated on the fourth floor. The use of it involved an extra payment. I think a rebate should have been made in consideration of the length of the two-way journey. I had not yet learnt to strike bargains with hotel managers in the bleak midwinter.

We did all the usual things: like visiting Versailles on a pouring wet day. There we were particularly impressed, under our present personal circumstances, by the bath, with hot and cold taps, en suite with the main bedroom, at the Petit Trianon. The guide announced that the uncovering of Pompeii, in 1752, had made baths fashionable. At the Louvre Joan pointed out the immense size of the feet of the Venus de Milo, larger than any man's. The fourteen hour train journey to Cannes was tedious. It was after ten at night when we arrived, very grateful to find Colonel and Mrs Carew on the platform to greet us.

La Bastide San Peyre was a pleasant villa on a hillside, four miles from Grasse. The sun shone warmly every day, but when it set, the stone-floored villa, insufficiently rugged, was very chilly. There was a third guest, a friend of a friend of Joyce, and hitherto unknown to her; a middle-aged spinster called Gordon Cumming. She incongruously united an air of, as Joyce expressed it, apologising for her existence, with a little manner of petty smugness.

Being a paying guest is a more complicated business than staying at an hotel. My bedroom's only access was through the bathroom that I shared with Miss Gordon Cumming. In spite of my assuring her that I would never enter the bathroom while she was in it, she behaved throughout as if she had some monstrous growth upon her body that I was determined, at all costs, to see. She would dither about in the passage to be certain when I left my bedroom. The two villas on either side of the Bastide were temporarily unoccupied by their owners. Joyce systematically cleared their gardens of every olive, which she sold to the olive mill at the bottom of the hill.

On Wednesday, February 6th, we were sitting on the terrace after lunch when Joyce went indoors to telephone to Lady Darnley, who lived with her husband about five miles away. We overheard her say, on the telephone: 'But how *awful!*' and debated, between ourselves, what could possibly have happened. The shock was considerable when Joyce returned to us and related that the Darnleys' gardener had rushed into their dining room, during lunch, to say that he had just heard on the wireless that the King of England was dead; had died in his sleep that morning. The attitude of the French was impressive, as I was to discover once more, when in France at the outbreak of the Falklands War in 1982. In February 1952 every paper made the subject front page news until after the funeral, every flag was at half mast and the tradesmen and shopkeepers all condoled with Joyce and expressed their sorrow.

4

THE SOCIETY OF SUTTON

I returned to England on February 16th, the day of the King's
funeral. Joan and Miss Gordon-Cumming stayed on at La
Bastide to irritate each other. The point of travel is to open
the windows of the mind and to come home refreshed, to a
renewed pleasure in the peace and comfort and the sense of
personal property of one's own home. I had enjoyed Joyce's
Devonian buccaneering spirit and the gift she had for getting to
know all the interesting people in the neighbourhood. Poor Miss
Gordon Cumming had been a dire warning of the result of giving
way to loneliness of the spirit. The alternative to loneliness,
however, presents recurring problems.

At this juncture I faced three. First, the love affair, if it can
be dignified by such a name. I was expected to yield myself, body
and soul, whenever himself chose to scamper in. To drop my
dustpan and brush and be taken at the foot of the stairs. In the
twenties there had been a popular song entitled 'In the Morning,
No'. It conveyed my sentiments exactly. Love-making, as by now
I had been superbly taught, takes a great deal of concentration and
spiritual as well as physical involvement. For women, the strong
passions aroused do not evaporate on the completion of the act.

Withdrawal, in every sense of that term, involves a sense of loss, frustration, finality.

Puritans can take pleasure from the thought that it is terribly difficult to find the opportunity to commit adultery; unless one goes deep into the woods, for which the British climate is most unsuited. At home the telephone bell or the doorbell invariably rang, with dramatic timing, within five minutes of the curtain rising. The cat made an entrance with a live bird or a mouse. My cottage stood in the middle of the village. Mrs Armstrong called for the savings money, Mrs Penfold with a tale of woe.

Vera Barry, the beautiful wife of Sir Gerald Barry, who lived nearly opposite, and was very dramatic herself, made fairly rare, but totally unheralded calls. I never really understood what she was talking about, but enjoyed watching the play of her flawless features as she talked. After my return from France, she saw on my mantelpiece a postcard of Clouet's picture of Gabrielle d'Estree and the Duchesse de Villars, naked, in a bath. Gabrielle d'Estree is fingering one of the Duchess's nipples. 'Oh, that *delightful* picture!' intoned Lady Barry, ardently. I told her: 'I saw it in Paris and was fascinated by it. I wrote and asked a friend, who is a history don at Oxford, what they were up to, but he replied that nobody knows.' Vera Barry gave no answer save a Mona Lisa smile, leaving me with the impression that feeling another woman in the bath is a sexual diversion known intimately to everybody but me and the clever men at Oxford.

The second problem on my plate was the re-emergence of my father into my life. My brother, John and his wife, Pamela, were now living in a house called New Grove, on the edge of Petworth. This was in some ways a plus, but the advantage was offset by my father rediscovering a pleasure in hunting, for the purpose of having the excuse to spend every weekend with them. They found this innovation immensely trying, as my father did not bother to listen to conversation, but, if it appeared to be entertaining others, he would interrupt to demand an explanation. This had to be detailed and exhaustive. At the end of each one my father announced, with disappointment: 'But that is very dull.' Nonetheless, he repeated the operation *ad nauseam*.

He admired his daughter-in-law immensely. She was perfect in every way: a renaissance of his wife, with added beauty. The fact that she was three inches taller than my mother had to be nullified by being transferred to me. For that purpose I ceased to be invisible to him. 'The tragedy about Ursula,' he informed the company, 'is that she is grotesquely tall. Pamela, now, is the perfect height.'

I protested that I am, in fact, half an inch shorter than Pamela. My father was derisive and begged me not to make such a fool of myself. 'How tall are you?' I asked Pamela. She pronounced clearly, looking straight at my father: 'Five foot, eleven.' He must have heard because, after looking stunned, he resumed his mono-logue on a different topic. I felt a lot of my old phobias returning.

One weekend, John hopefully suggested that my father might prefer to return to London after hunting on Saturday, as he would otherwise find himself having lunch alone on Sunday, John and Pamela having been invited to lunch at Arundel Castle. My father, while ignoring the idea that he should go home on Saturday evening, asked, with interest, 'Do you know the Duke of Norfolk?' His son, with heavy sarcasm, replied that every week the Norfolks put the names of all their neighbours into a hat, then drew out a certain number and asked those names to lunch. My father had no difficulty in taking this statement seriously and replied that he had always heard that Norfolk was a very good man in the county.

The third problem was that, as my herd of goats increased, one half of the coal shed, which had never been ideal quarters, became utterly insufficient for their needs. They began to overflow into makeshift sheds in the back garden. Herding them to pasture had always been a restricting tie. Much as the life in, and the society of, Sutton suited me, I felt that I must try and find a cottage with some grazing land attached. Meantime a kind local farmer, Mr Neale, offered me a rough field on the foothills of the downs. It was ideal goat pasture, being composed mostly of weeds and brambles. Access involved loading the goats into the van, driving them as near to the downs as possible, and then walking them up a bridle path, known as Puck Street, that ascended the downs, beside which lay my field. The problem was to make it goat-proof with electric fencing.

In April 1952 my uncle Charles Leconfield, the last private owner of Petworth House, died. Leaving my brother 30,000 Sussex acres to administer, as part of an even larger inheritance, most of 80,000 acres, which had reluctantly to be sold to settle death duties. My uncle had for a long time been senile and the Estate was severely run-down, neglected and deeply in debt. My brother, with no interest in the intricacies of rural life and finance, found himself, by reason of his birthright, trapped, as it were, upon a desert island, from which only death could release him, and, until that event occurred, on his fifty second birthday, the pressures and responsibilities mounted with the years.

Not least of them were our parents. My father had allowed his claims, with those of an elder brother, to be bypassed to his son to save treble death duties. Nonetheless he felt that the show was his: that is the trappings, the prestige, the hospitality, without a thought to the problems. My brother and sister-in-law refused none of the onerous demands made on them to make Petworth House available to the parents who looked on it as their own. Yet the restrictions dictated by reason and necessity evoked in my father a querulous wail of childish deprivation for all to hear. There are people alive today who, without bothering to acquaint themselves with the obverse side of the coin, still blame my brother for ill-treating his aged father by failing to give way to his more demented whims.

With regard to fencing the field, I knew of nobody who could do this job and, for lack of an alternative, turned to my brother for help. A completely incomprehensible state of affairs was then explained. Although John owned the estate, as it was a Company, he could not order any employee to do an outside job, as he would have to pay for it. I had already assembled the fencing materials, and the idea presented that the whereabouts of every single man is known to a nicety through out every hour of every day did not make sense to me. I was told that my ignorance compared with that of Winifred, Duchess of Portland, who had carried out some immense building project at Welbeck. When friends cried: 'Goodness, it must have cost a lot!' she replied: 'No, that's what's so lovely. It cost absolutely nothing. It was all done by the estate.'

Shortly afterwards I heard, through the grapevine, of two brothers, called Baker, who went about doing any job that was needed and were highly skilled. The Baker brothers were invaluable to me for the next twenty years. John generously offered to pay their bill, as they were not working for his Company, but their charges were so reasonable that I was well able to decline his thoughtful offer.

Family funerals in this century have invariably been hilarious get-togethers, where friends and relations, often meeting once more, after a lengthy absence, have gathered together the threads of family life with pleasurable reminiscence of things said in times past. I hope my own will be of this nature. At Uncle Charles's funeral, my younger sister-in-law, Anne, turned to me at the chattering lunch party, before our uncle was consigned to the vault, and exclaimed: 'Oh Ursula, I do think it is pathetic. I know Uncle Charles wasn't a particularly nice old man, but here we all are, these people, and none of them sad, none of them minding, not a tear in anybody's eye. Just think if it was one of us popping off, and nobody caring a bit.'

In the next year, 1953, I left Sutton and John and Pamela moved into the south end of Petworth House. Pamela in time-honoured fashion, started putting her personal imprint on the interior decoration, to the intense horror of my mother, who, while I am sure she would have done the same according to her own style, deeply resented her daughter-in-law getting the opportunity she was deprived of.

Pamela was an amusing purveyor of the more bizarre events of their social life. Such as staying with Judy Montagu at a house in Suffolk, so haunted that guests were flung bodily from their beds; a hearse arrived at the door at unforeseen times and to catch the driver's eye spelled death. The last time she and John had stayed with Miss Montagu they had not got a wink of sleep on account of prowling footsteps in the room above. When they had complained of their ordeal the next day, cold water was metaphorically flung on what must be their overheated imagination, since the room in question had been kept locked since the butler committed suicide in it.

It was fortunate that my brother and sister-in-law were impervious to psychic phenomena at home, since their guests complained of having suffered similar chilling experiences at New Grove. Lady Lambton had been overcome by the haunted atmosphere pervading the house and how doors mysteriously opened of their own accord. As in Suffolk, she had been aware of a great thumping and bumping overhead while in her bedroom. Pamela mentioned these, to her unexperience causes for alarm, to her aunt, Olein Wyndham-Quin, who then divulged that she had the frequent impression of there being unseen people going up and down the staircase, but that the atmosphere was, none the less, not a frightening one.

When Pamela had tea with two old women who had lived in Petworth all their lives, they questioned her closely as to whether she was happy, contented, at ease at New Grove and finally admitted that the house was supposed to be horribly haunted. A baby had been murdered and there was a blocked-up room where a duel had been fought, leaving the floor covered in blood. A new floor had been laid, but at once the bloodstains had appeared again. The floor had therefore been removed and the room blocked up, but access could still be gained to it through a window in the roof. As is usual with such stories, the narrators were vague about dates and details and those who might have supplied supporting evidence were unfortunately in their graves.

We did surge up to the roof in a biting wind and found the room. It was indeed above the bedroom that Lady Lambton had occupied. The floor boards were gone, leaving only the joists, the windows had been blocked up, except the one that admitted access from the tiles and any communicatory staircase from the rest of the house had been removed. There remained a fireplace at the end of the room.

Regarding my personal affairs, I thought, wrongly as it turned out, that I had been unusually lucky in finding a cottage with one and a half acres of land near Graffham, a secluded village, leading nowhere, at the foot of the downs between Petworth and Midhurst. It had a broody house for hens that the invaluable Baker boys could convert into goat pens. The cottage stood back from the road, behind a hedge, in a secluded lane. It was not totally isolated. There was a cottage on the other side of the road, just beyond mine, and yet another about a hundred yards further on. In the opposite direction, across the road, were two more houses, screened by trees. The occupier of one of these latter houses had approached me on one of my frequent surveying forays to the cottage prior to moving in. I was somewhat alarmed by him and his inquisitive enquiries, delivered in a foreign accent. His appearance had a brigandish quality and I felt that he might well be one of those who murdered lonely women, cut them up into neat sections, and buried the bits in different places. In fact he turned out to be by far the kindest and sanest of the somewhat peculiar people who inhabited the other residences. His foreign accent was Scottish.

A great many people came to visit Brown's House. The first was Mr White of the estate agents, Whitehead and Whitehead, to take particulars. 'I suppose you call this the drawing room?' he said.

I told him: 'No. I think that drawing room is too grand a term. I call it the sitting room.'

'As long as you don't call it the lounge,' Mr White declared firmly.

'I most certainly do not; but I am surprised that you don't. It appears to be a house agent's favourite word.'

'Not,' stated Mr White, 'in our firm. The boss issued a circular only the other day saying that he regretted to notice that there were far too many lounges getting into the advertisements and the less this vulgar and dreadful word was used the better.'

When the potential buyers arrived in large numbers, they invariably regretted that the cottage had not three bedrooms. With mounting asperity I enquired why, in that case, they had bothered to view it at all. The answer was that they hoped it might be a comparatively simple matter to add on an extra room. The shape and situation of Brown's House did not favour this dream.

I became involved in the world of builders, plumbers, furniture removers — playing one lot off against another, seeking the most favourable financial terms. A man from Pickfords came to give a furniture removal estimate in the morning, and a man from Farrs of Chichester in the afternoon. The Pickfords man was young and came on a motor cycle. He asked no questions, glanced briefly at each room and then quoted £8. I informed him that I was expecting Farrs representative later, and he commented: 'Ah, Farrs are a funny lot. One never knows where one is with them. One day they might quote £15 and the next day £5.'

I remarked fervently that I hoped today would be their £5 day. We got into conversation and, in no time, were deep into labour conditions, politics, newspapers and comedians. We discovered that we were as one in liking Laurel and Hardy and Arthur English and failing to be amused by Ted Ray and Abbot and Costello. He had been shocked by somebody writing to a newspaper to divulge that, on their days off, the writer, his wife and the children all went off in different directions.

'I wouldn't enjoy a holiday,' explained my new acquaintance, 'unless the wife was with me. I don't even like going to the cinema alone. You see, I've got this awful laugh and when something in the picture amuses me, I see people looking disapprovingly at me. If my wife is there, I don't care.'

Farrs' man was elderly. He asked several questions, spent quite a time in each room and then said that he would post the estimate. I said briskly that there was no time for that. I was moving on Friday. He pointed out that he was only the estimate maker; the price fixing was done by somebody else, but if I insisted, he could give me a rough estimate. He pored over his notebook for a while and came up with the figure of £15! I had, indeed, caught him on the wrong day.

Besides myself, there was my poodle, Sancho, and my ginger cat, Panza, who would be moving to Graffham, along with the goats. But there was a third member of the household to be considered. For a year or more a very small mouse had been sharing the kitchen. It bustled about in my presence, quite unconcerned, and once I found it sitting in a spoon in the cutlery drawer. One day Panza caught it. I chased him up the stairs and down again, until he dropped it. I picked the mouse up and it seemed unharmed. I left a piece of bacon rind under the stove, and the next day it was gone. A greater tragedy struck a day or so later. I found my mouse drowned in a jug of milky water that I had used to rinse the separator. I was deeply distressed, but it solved the mouse-moving problem.

The Sunday before, Lord Mersey, as if to give me a good send off, had surpassed himself. As we came out of church, he approached me in the porch. 'I hoped to see you today, as I have a rather improper poem I would like to read to you.'

I was not prepared for him to extract from his pocket, then and there, a typewritten sheet of paper. As we walked down the path to the gate he proceeded to declaim, in stentorian tones, with the entire congregation following us, a series of verses headed, in capital letters, 'Lament of a Heifer on giving Birth to a Calf by Artificial Insemination'. The subject was treated with unflagging bawdiness, but was not side-splittingly funny, which, in view of the circumstances, was just as well. The last lines went something like:

> And those land-girl tarts
> Play with our parts
> And have all the fun that we miss.

5

THE GROTESQUES OF GRAFFHAM

I moved to my new home in Graffham on March 27th 1953. The removal firm sent four lunatics with the van. Their first act was to take the front door off its hinges in such a way that, when they replaced it, the door would neither open nor shut. They cut the electric light flexes, rather than draw the plugs out of the sockets and, at Graffham, they made a pile of the furniture in the middle of the kitchen, and prepared to go. In the three years that I had lived on my own one of the most important lessons I had learnt was not to pay for any job in advance. I brought the lunatics to their senses by explaining that not one penny would be paid unless they arranged the furniture in its proper order.

Graffham introduced me to middle-class attitudes. A point of view, or rather of non-thinking and -seeing, that I had never encountered before and have spent much time side-stepping since. The people that I had known and mixed with at Sutton were intellectual or sporting or country folk. I felt equally at ease with all three and shared the same values. Graffham was a haven for retired professional people, including widows and spinsters, who were all waiting for death; with what degree of resignation or anticipation, I doubt if they questioned. Questions, deductions,

speaking of people behind their back, admitting to being neurotic
or foul-minded, were all ill-bred. To behave correctly and have
everything daintily served, were the only standards that mattered.
Conversation must, on no account, arouse such dangerous
emotions as ideas. One spoke of the weather, of how one hated
shopping, which shops one hated shopping in, with comparisons
of shoppers' opinions of this item or that. This led, quite naturally,
to individual recipes for scones, with reference to what one of the
company's mother had always said. What the dead had always said
was quoted so frequently that one came to be able to silently
mouth the words along with the speaker. Where the inhabitants
of Sutton had met round the lunch or supper table, Graffham only
entertained at tea-time.

In December I report one of several such tea parties, because
there were elements in it that struck renewed terror in my now
definitely neurotic mind.

I had tea with an old girl called Mrs Spicer, widow of a
Petworth doctor. She was nice and cosy, if not particularly
interesting. Another woman was there, who I thought must
live with her: a large, toothy, cheerful spinster. It was
immensely pleasant to find an ageing spinster here who was
cheerful. She was the only one present. The other two were
Miss Sutherland and her cousin Miss 'Teddie' Flaxman. The
latter a fat woman, who looked fortyish seen from the side
and fiftyish full face. Her hair was arranged in heavy Edwardian
curls on the forehead and caught up into more curls, tied by
a ribbon, high at the back of her head. She had silly, affected
mannerisms and said to me: 'You *sell* your milk? But who
to? What do they *do* with it?'

My reply: 'I've no reason to suppose "they" throw it on
the rubbish heap. I daresay you'll hardly believe it, but I
understand "they" drink it,' did not disconcert her in the least.

I cannot imagine how Miss Sutherland tolerated her,
because Miss S. was clearly intelligent. Withdrawn, small,
neat and well-bred looking, she spoke little and her face, in
repose, had an air of gloomy sadness. When she spoke, her
eyes flashed a humour which was not reflected in her words.
Describing the acting of Michael Redgrave and Peggy Ashcroft

in *Antony and Cleopatra*, she said that they acted to the roof, they flung everything they had into their parts and yet they left one with the impression that neither noticed that the other was there. This acute observation was wasted on the company, including myself. It was years since I had been to the theatre. Anyway I was too busily engaged in drinking her in.

I ended my report: 'Miss S. is the editress of *Woman's Journal* and two other periodicals. She goes to all the first nights and knows many interesting people — and yet that unsatisfied gloom. Oh, how terrible!'

Later, I nerved myself to ring up Miss Sutherland and suggest that she and the terrible 'Teddie' should come to tea with me. I neither drank nor ate tea myself, but Graffham's conforming standards pressed, like shackles, on the freedom of my spirit. Miss Sutherland said, as one who laid down the rules, 'I think it would be more suitable if you came to tea with us — sometime. Goodbye.'

It had been hoped that the remoteness of the cottage at Graffham would prove idyllic for love-making, but Graffham's passion for the elixir of a cup of tea ruined this hallucinatory dream. William had a nodding acquaintance with Mr and Mrs Jackson who lived a hundred yards up the road. After our first revelry in this new bower, we descended the stairs, he flushed, I dishevelled, to see Mr Jackson approaching the door, with the jocular information that he had just happened to be passing and recognised the car standing at the door. He had therefore walked down my drive to suggest that we join him and his wife for a cup of tea.

It might have been psychologically prudent to accept. By refusing, both of us were subjected subsequently, at the chance meetings that Fate knows so well how to bring about, to a barrage of interrogation by Mrs Jackson: 'Fancy us knowing each other! How long had we been friends? Did we see much of each other?' To minds attuned to nothing beyond weather and shopping, it was natural that the sudden introduction of a wider concept of human behaviour should be obsessive; but it scared the wits out of both of us, especially since his car, standing in the main street at Sutton, had never evoked the faintest interest. We neither of us wanted any hint of publicity.

My life now degenerated, by degrees — nobody ever hurried in Graffham — into a waste of agonising doubts, hopes, fears and waning expectancy.

When he did visit me, on subsequent occasions, the looked-forward-to sense of freedom of self-expression, freedom from the fear of interruption and public notice, was yet again denied us. The Jacksons seemed to be keeping a constant vigil on my house. Wherever we met them individually it was: 'So William was with you again. I thought of looking in. I wanted to ask him about the Point-to-Point . . .' And to him 'It is always nice to see you. I suppose you'll be calling on Ursula now.' I daresay it was largely that there was so little in which to take an interest within the parish of Graffham. I, too, was very conscious of being denied the social contacts I had enjoyed with all the inhabitants of Sutton. I had also become increasingly responsive to the needs of the latent sensuosity that I found I possessed. Without the regular opportunity to satisfy it and lacking the knowledge and experience to cope with the situation, the result was a sense of utter loneliness and unfulfilment that I found appalling.

I made the discovery that the phrase 'wringing one's hands' is not just a mode of speech. It really happens. At intervals throughout each dreary day I burst into hysterical sobs and wandered from room to room, wringing my hands. I, who had learnt not to bother about my personality, my status as a woman, my human needs, now looked, with fear and trepidation and a ghastly sense of identity, at the ageing female nonentities who were my neighbours.

Ashamed of the scenes that I found myself unable to avoid making, I suggested that he and I no longer met. At least that would dispense with the frequently unrewarded expectancy. 'After all,' I pointed out, consciously realistic, 'it is not as though you loved me.'

'I like being with you,' he told me, 'and you excite me.'

Excite him! This was an extraordinary thing for my father's daughter to be told. Not even Marlene Dietrich excited men as God had made her. Before she was capable of doing that the Make-Up Department had to get hold of her: crimp her hair, dye it and paint her face and lips. Then the Dress Department took the job over and dressed her in black stockings and tights. It remained for the Director to set her up against a bar and have her enquire huskily what the boys in the back room would have. That was what getting men excited was about. Doing what comes naturally must be something else. But what? At Graffham I failed to find out.

Nearly opposite to my house lived Mr and Mrs Beard. Mrs Beard wrote cookery articles for a women's magazine and made pastry in batches. When I called at her door — and when frantic with loneliness one will call on almost anybody, she invariably announced brightly: 'I've just got a nice batch of pastry in the oven.' On my suggesting that pastry is at its best when fresh, she looked at me, startled and uncomprehending. Mr Beard never spoke, to his wife or anybody else. He reserved his particular Cold Comfort Farm role for letter writing. One January day I took the goats for a walk. Two days later I was favoured by a letter from Mr Beard.

> I am most interested by your passage through our place this
> afternoon (Tuesday). No doubt there must be a public
> footpath with which you are acquainted and with which I am,
> as yet, unaware, being very much a recent arrival. When you
> have time to spare I would regard it as a favour if you would
> call and point out to me the course of the path, so that I can
> set about the provision of a proper right of way.

This extraordinary letter, penned by one compared with whom the Starkadders appeared positively normal, referred not to my passage through his hall and garden, but returning from a walk with six goats in attendance, through a copse and across a field, at least fifty yards from his house. All my life I had been accustomed to proceed, on foot and on horseback, across man's heritage of the countryside; carefully closing gates, not disturbing cattle, avoiding sown crops, rejoicing in being close to nature.

I went to consult the police. The entire Force was at a conference, two female clerks informed me. At a later date I was more fortunate. Trespassing without damage, I was told, as I had expected, does not come within police jurisdiction. Mr Beard was entitled to take civil action against me, but whether he would obtain any satisfaction was moot and would depend on the mood of the magistrate.

It is possible that Mr Beard was directly descended from William the Conqueror. When taking some goats to Lyndhurst Show, I stopped in the New Forest to let the goats graze. At once three foresters leapt out of the brushwood and ordered me to leave the place. I remarked that things did not seem to have changed much since William the Conqueror's time. The foresters assured me that, in the enclosed areas, they hadn't.

A month after I arrived the vicar called, with his wife and their rather tiresome child, aged about two. I have no notion what he thought of me, but I found him a most interesting study. He never smiled, but occasionally gave a short bark of a laugh, as if the effort involved hurt him. His whole personality seemed entombed in such stark misery that he could not fail to interest me. The church was always full and he put great life into his services: repeating the prayers as if their meaning was momentous and keeping the service short and concise. He preached fairly long sermons, but he had a gift of holding one's interest and attention. What intrigued me was that his sermons were invariably on the theme of finding inner peace and fulfilment in life. Could he, I wondered, ever listen to himself? While I listened to his sermons, I did not, as it were, absorb them, from the inescapable conviction that, as they clearly hadn't done anything for his innate unhappiness, there could be nothing there to mitigate mine.

I did get to know one agreeably eccentric old girl, called Miss Wilberforce, a direct descendant of the man who gave his life to achieving the abolition of the slave trade. She lived, in witch-like seclusion, on the edge of a wood and asked me had I given any thought to what action I would take if burglars were to break in? I admitted that I had not got around to considering the matter. Miss Wilberforce had it all worked out. She would open her bedroom window and clang a handbell into the night air. As she had no neighbours within sight, I expressed concern that such an action might incite the burglar to do her physical harm. Miss

Wilberforce remained convinced of the efficacy of her plan. Seen from the bell, book and candle angle, she may well have had a point. I asked her over to meet Lord and Lady Mersey. Lady Mersey was indisposed on the day.

When I introduced Miss Wilberforce to Lord Mersey, they looked at each other with mutual ill-favour and said that they were already acquainted. Miss Wilberforce and I were both reading Lady Emily Lutyen's autobiography, *A Blessed Girl*. I remarked, with amazement, on Lady Emily's revelation that her mother's head had, on occasion, been lice-ridden. Lord Mersey and Miss Wilberforce confessed that, not only had their parents' heads been in a similar condition, so had their own. Lord Mersey then remarked: 'If you will excuse me for saying so, you have the longest legs of any woman I have ever met.' He was gazing at my limbs as he spoke, and the Graffham miasma was by now so strong in me that, instinctively I hastened to straighten my legs and draw my skirt down over them.

Jack James, a cousin by marriage used to stay the occasional weekend, bringing a whiff of the wider world beyond. Once he told how he had been to Paris for the wedding of the American Ambassador's daughter. In a cafe he had got into conversation with a lugubrious Briton who had come to Paris in search of sexual diversion, only to find that General de Gaulle had closed down all the brothels. Jack, delighted to appear in the guise of the sophisticated Englishman abroad, had supplied him with some addresses and a few useful phrases to repeat to waiters. In return the man had shown him a photograph of his early Georgian house near Newbury, with the information that Newbury was a second Sodom and that the mayor and several notable citizens were involved.

It was easier to control the self-pity that I was so rightly ashamed of, during the cold winters, when every ounce of energy went into keeping warm and preventing the water pipes from permanently freezing. Snow drifted against the garage door and froze. The snow plough and the sand sprayer did not bother about the cul-de-sac road to Graffham. The coal lorry could not get through. I was fortunate in having a loyal casual worker to do the heavy outside work, in one Mr Hamilton, who cycled over from the neighbouring village of Selham in all weathers. Mr Hamilton cut down an apple tree and chopped it into logs when the coal supply ran out. It became moot whether he might have to cut down a second one, but fortunately the long-awaited thaw came in the nick of time.

Mr Hamilton had the true countryman's disdain for the conventions involved in the unwritten rules of high society. 'Supposing,' he instanced, 'that I was asked to dinner at Arundel Castle, I'd get all muddled up about what I was supposed to do with those serviettes and things.' While reflecting that the Jacksons and the Beards and the widows and spinsters would sell their souls for an invitation from the Duke and Duchess of Norfolk, I replied: 'For starters, you'd find the Duke would call the serviettes napkins.'

'There you are!' claimed Mr Hamilton, triumphantly, having proved his point concerning the unnecessary trappings of social intercourse at the highest level.

6

THE SMALL GREEN CAR

When the roads were clear again, I was grateful for any outings that provided a broader social horizon than could be found in Graffham. My mother was a friend of Lady Meade-Fetherstonehaugh of Uppark, near South Harting. Uppark, of moderate size, is one of the most beautiful houses in Europe. From its windows the downland landscape, varied by clumps of trees, stretches unchanged since the eighteenth century, to the coast. My mother considered Meg Meade nice, but boring. I found her vitality invigorating, while recognising that her special form of autocracy would clash with that of my mother. Meg's religious faith was deceptively simple. God was present, at her elbow, nodding approval of all her opinions. Therefore, if you disagreed with Lady Meade, on any level, you disagreed with God. As God did not play bridge, nor inhabit the social scene, my mother naturally found any reference to Him boring.

One afternoon, having tea at Uppark, I was refreshed to find there a most unGraffham-like spinster: Miss Amy Stokes from South Harting. Miss Stokes was middle-aged, good-looking, confident and composed. She did not seem aware of her miserable condition and was, consequently, much better company for me than, say, Miss Sutherland. I had just been confessing to Meg and Miss Stokes how deadly I found neighbours and Meg was showing incredulous surprise, when a Mr and Mrs C. from Rogate, stepped into the room. Within five minutes I could scarce forebear to utter the words: 'See what I mean!' but Meg appeared to find Mr C., at least, delighful. Conversation started stickily. Mrs C. revealed that she had been in Italy recently which always made her so sad; there was such a tremendous sense of the past about Italy. The same was true of Paris. She knew that it was called gay — and so it was, in a way, but also so dreadfully sad. I kept silent from fear of appearing snubbing, but Miss Stokes announced blandly that she, also, was aware of the past in Paris, but she felt nothing depressing about such an atmosphere.

Miss Stokes also happened to say a propos of something or other, that it was so lucky that we had a Queen on the throne, in times like the present. 'Oh, not lucky,' cried Meg. 'God-given!'

'Very well,' allowed Miss Stokes, 'God given,' although God did not always give when one wanted Him to. I warmed more and more to this admirable woman.

We spoke of the members of Parliament voting themselves more money. I said that I had listened to a discussion between Sir Edward Boyle and Anthony Wedgewood-Benn, who acknowledged that they were lucky enough to have private incomes. Many Socialist MPs who had not, could not stand the pace, and it would seriously cramp the House of Commons if only people with private incomes could become MPs. Mr C. came out with the only comment worthy of recollection that I heard him make that afternoon, namely that he doubted if many MPs would be considered worth an equal salary in any other job they might apply for.

After this outing I hoped that I'd wake up feeling happier the next morning. But it was not to be. I spent the day determinedly telling myself that my feelings were of no importance and it presented an opportunity to be seized not to think of myself. I was searching for another cottage to move to. Apart from the loneliness of Graffham, the one and a half acres were proving insufficient to sustain six goats. As, not surprisingly, a cottage with a sizeble amount of land was not to be found, my brother,

John, kindly offered a patch of his newly acquired 30,000 acres to build on. This plan was held up for over a year not only by the complicated proceedings with the Planning Authority, but by the implacable opposition of John's agent, who, having run his own show, unhindered, through the years of our uncle's decline, was continuing, with some success, while paying lip service to his new employer, in preventing any infringements of his infallible rights.

On July 2nd of that year of 1954 there was held, at Petworth House, the most elite and superbly staged party to be given since the visit of the Allied Sovereigns in 1814. On that occasion the Tsar, Alexander of Russia, had left his Cossacks camped on the green at Chiddingfold, where their savage demeanour and incredible riding feats had induced a nervous young woman to have a miscarriage on the spot. The present celebration was not without its turmoil. The motive was a ball, given by Pamela's uncle, Lord Dunraven, for his daughters, Caroline and Melissa Wyndham-Quin. His American wife had many European connections, who came over from the Continent for the occasion. The royal families of England and France were represented by Princess Alexandra and the son of the Comte de Paris, who signed the visitors' book 'Henri de France.' Tiaras were worn and afterwards the European contingent confessed to having been impressed by the beauty of the English women and the magnificence of their jewelry, surpassing anything to be seen on the Continent.

My younger brother, Mark, and his wife, Anne, represented a segment of the teething troubles that are part of the preparations for any great event. Anne rang me up to ask if I had received an invitation card to the dinner that was to precede the ball? I replied that I had. It appeared that Anne and Mark had not. I offered to bring this to Pamela's notice next time I saw her. Anne asked me not to. She did not want to appear to be making an undue family fuss. In reply to my mother's next 'what's the news?' call, I included this item, adding Mark and Anne's wish that it should not be referred to. Undoubtedly my mother was jealous that Pamela was occupying the post of chatelaine of Petworth that, my mother considered, but for a cruel stroke of fate, should rightfully be hers. My information gave her the opportunity to deliver a two-pronged attack, using her own peculiar brand of offensiveness, to her sensitive daughter-in-law. In reply to Pamela's explanation that she and her aunt, Nancy Dunraven, had both issued verbal invitations to dinner, so what of it if the reminder cards had become delayed? my mother informed her, in tones of sympathetic suffering, that, there it was, Anne and Mark were so understandably hurt that they would not now be coming to the ball at all. How could they? Without a card they might be denied admittance. It was rather hard, to motor all the way from Kent and then to have to prepare dinner for themselves.

Expostulation under attack was, as I very well knew, of no avail. My mother proceeded to move in with a well-aimed death blow, delivered from behind. 'Now that you are established at Petworth House,' she enquired in deceptively silky tones 'Have you no sugar basins there?'

Caught off guard and puzzled, Pamela assured her: 'Yes, of course.' My mother snapped: 'In that case, perhaps you will return to me the one I lent you.'

On the day of the ball the continuing uncertainty and sense of general hopelessness regarding the relationship between William and myself combined to put me in the most vulnerable of moods. I approached Petworth House striving to attain some degree of calm, however superficial. The spectacle was sensational enough. Beautiful flower clusters in every room. Clumps of trees in the park floodlit. A sparkling fountain built upon the lake. To my naive surprise the acquaintances of my youth: Angie Laycock, Virginia Sykes, Susan Askew, greeted me with warm friendliness. Anne introduced me to two of the outstanding beauties: Jane, Countess of Westmorland and Lady Caroline Gilmour, whose spontaneous charm was reassuring. I thought Caroline Gilmour's tiara the finest of the many splendid ones that sparkled on every married woman's head.

Sixty-eight people dined in the marble Hall. I sat between Pamela's father, Val Wyndham-Quin, and Hugh Fraser. I found the latter a curious character; easy to talk to, but with a heartless quality that prevented affinity in discourse. He did not dance with me. I was too humble to take offence at that, but felt that it was not entirely necessary for him to give an elaborate start whenever we encountered one another in the course of the evening, while informing everyone within hearing that he had it on his conscience that he had not yet danced with this woman, an omission he had every intention of repairing at a later and undisclosed period.

Cinderella left between midnight and one o'clock, but Anne and Mark stayed till the end. I was awake when they returned after 5 am, and they wandered in and out of my bedroom as they undressed, discussing the ball with all the pleasure that Jane Austen, in *Mansfield Park*, assigns to such recollections. It had been an unqualified success and the floor had been still crowded at the end.

Anne was very sympathetic to my locational dilemma. She told me that I must speak to John of my great need for the plot of land currently under dispute amd to point out that my whole happiness depended on acquiring it. I reflected that perhaps if my whole happiness did depend upon nothing more than that, I would take my courage in both hands in my own interests. Life at Petworth would undoubtedly be pleasanter and less isolated, but would not fulfil the overwhelming need of love and usefulnes that I increasingly craved and that, on account of which, I was foolish enough to let myself wallow in indifference to any other aspect of life.

I also felt reluctant to add to John's burdens in view of the increasing strain and harassment he was under from our parents. They had, as usual, received several invitations for August and had refused them all. Instead my mother informed John and Pamela that she and my father intended to spend the month of August at Petworth House. It was explained to them that the redecorating, which had been temporarily held up by the ball, was to be completed in August, when the rooms at the private end of the house would be available, during the absence of John and Pamela, for the painters and wall-paperers to move in. My parents, without a tremor, then demanded that New Grove, which was standing bare and empty, should be refurnished, recarpeted, recurtained and a resident staff assembled, solely for the purpose of making a fact of their compulsive whim. It can be imagined that, while failing in the accomplishment, my mother's unique gift for psychological annihilation had left my brother and sister-in-law equally shattered.

Subconsciously, since I made no record of it in my diary, I was seeking what I needed. As the one and a half acres were proving insufficient pasturage for six goats, I was forced to herd them by the roadside again. Every afternoon a small green car hurtled past, never slackening speed. The man at the wheel looked impatient at his way being cluttered with goats, and causing those goats to use all their natural agility to avoid a horrid death beneath the wheels of his car. I asked Mr Hamilton if he knew who this would-be assassin was? 'Oh, that will be Colonel Halton who manages the Stud,' was the answer. 'His wife,' added Mr Hamilton, 'is the most disagreeable woman I have ever seen. Whenever I go to Midhurst, there she is at the corner of the street, glowering at people.' They seemed a well-matched pair.

Next time the little green car scattered my goats, I shook my fist at it. The time after it slowed down and the occupant, a man I judged to be in his late fifties, stopped and spoke to me. He had an elegant, well-bred appearance and an attractive voice. From then on he always stopped for a chat. I thought him rather a stupid man; he appeared only able to speak freely on the subject of horses: their breeding and their performance. On the other hand there was nobody more interesting to talk to. I took to mugging-up the information on the sporting page of the Times. Fortunately their racing correspondent at that time had a rare gift with words. I read his column with pleasure for the way he expressed himself and it was therefore easy to remember what he had written. This made verbal intercourse with the driver of the green car a great deal easier. He was always promising to show me the mares and foals at the Stud, but never did. Finally I pointed out that these civil invitations were, in fact, meaningless. After that I visited the Stud twice a year. There is a limit to what you can say about twenty to thirty thoroughbred mares, none of which are down on their pasterns, weak in the shoulder or sloping too much behind the saddle.

Instead I looked at their manager. He was tall and lean, if

thickset, with the military bearing and easy carriage of the vocational cavalryman, and the slight unconscious swagger which often goes with those who are accustomed to effortlessly mount a horse. What I also noticed, with a certain amount of consternation, was that, in spite of thinking him dull, I was subtly aware that he was possessed of that indefinable power: animal magnetism. Dull or not, I ached to go to bed with him.

To the many who appear to be unacquainted with this potent aphrodisiac, it pertains to a strong physical attraction quite unconnected to mutual attitudes of mind. It is not transient. Whatever the victim's subsequent mental feelings connected to the male animal magnetism, she will remain aware of that maddeningly powerful attraction, even if she has come to hate its possessor. Does it lie at the root of the adage: 'Hell hath no fury like a woman scorned'?

What further fascinated me was that my new friend treated certain of the mares like adored women: stroking them, kissing them and calling them by every expression of endearment. This behaviour was made more potent in that he shared with William the alert eye contact and had that dulcet tone of voice that could, and did when he wished it, assume the bewitching cadence of the practised, if discreet, philanderer.

And all these charms were being wasted on horses: dissatisfied, seeking some intangible goal, with a dawning consciousness that I was capable of eliciting sexual responses, these observations gradually served to put me on my mettle. A man who appeared to find equine females superior to the human species needed to be taken in hand. In hindsight I am amazed that it never entered my thick head to invite him in for a drink on his way home.

The Times, in those days, was more helpful than merely in the literary ability of its racing correspondent. Am I the only one of its readers who regrets that it has dropped the Personal Column as a means of inquiry and communication? I studied this column daily, not infrequently finding food for speculation in the realms of human interest and concern. A bleak mood was lightened by the following entry: 'Will Miss Durden consider again the post of Help Companion. This time lamp incident no obstacle.' The letters section was also more fruitful in the area of human endeavour. A

Mrs Talbot wrote suggesting that enterprising clergymen should hold services before the buses were due to start on Sunday excursions. The Rev. Whiteley hastened to reply that he had done just that; and what was the result? All the Bad People took the window seats while the Good People were taking part in the Service. I wrote to the Editor, remarking that, if the Rev. Whiteley was doing his job properly, he should have sent off his congregation so inculcated with the Christian Spirit that to allow others to have the best seats would add considerably to the pleasure of the day. The goats would also be feeling satisfied, on account of having shown superior cunning in competition with the sheep. In this simple and innocent way a good time was ensured for all.

7

HOW TO NAME A HOUSE

When John raised the subject of this 'Khubla Khan thing of yours' I knew it was the light at the end of the tunnel. People enthuse: 'Oh, how lovely to build your own house. You can have everything as you want it.' They are wrong. All you can have is what the architect wants. The design is a work of his personal imagination and artistic skill. To have the Philistine client making any criticism cuts him to the quick and he hurriedly dons his business hat to nip such pretensions in the bud. Apart from that my objective faculties were fully engaged and I shuttled almost daily between Petworth and Graffham in a state of business-like absorption.

I had one interesting conversation before I left Graffham. There was a nice woman called Lady Ricardo living in the village at that time. Her grandsons took an interest in my goats and, on two occasions, appeared upon my scene. They were escorted by their father, Dr. Bertram, of the Polar Research Institute, which, to my astonishment, he informed me was situated in the temperate zone of Cambridge.

To the lay mind, everything to do with polar research appeared to be highly unexpected. England had no ships suitable for polar voyages, since steel is more vulnerable to ice than wood. This country had to hire suitable vessels, when it wanted them, from Norway. Canada and the United States were in the course of building for themselves an arctic navy. Greenland, he told me was going through a mild period, comparable to that when it was peopled by Norsemen from the twelfth to the fifteenth centuries. By the fifteenth century a chilly climate had developed and the Norsemen died out, due to this and the Hanseatic League which, I might remember, came to an end about that time. I had to honestly confess that I did not remember, never having previously heard of the Hanseatic League. With all my heart I wish I had applied to Dr. Bertram for enlightenment on this subject. Since that time the Hanseatic League has constantly cropped up in my reading and nobody to whom I have applied has been able to tell me anything of its functions.

Huskies have always appeared to me to be dogs of great charm, looks and intelligence. So that I was horrified to be told that it is customary to take about a hundred of these dogs on polar explorations; and then shoot them, for their pains, at the end of the trip. Impossible to bring them home because of quarantine; impossible to return them to whence they came because of transport difficulties. About twelve, I was relieved to hear, had been brought back from the last expedition, to go on the permanent strength of those maintained in the Falkland Islands.

If you build a house you have to find a name for it. That this is a well-nigh insuperable problem is proved by the number of deplorable names displayed, on slices of wood, on the wall or gate of so many homesteads. I put my problem to Henry Halton during one of our roadside chats. For me it was a welcome change from a discussion of a horse that had run in the 2.30 at Sandown. He was a man who took everything with calm. I suppose you do when it has been your profession to face shot and shell and, also, an immense number of women, most of whom had husbands in the background. He said a solution might be found by going through the stallion list. He produced this manual and started quoting from it. When he reached the name 'Honeyway' I stopped him. It had an agreeably evocative sound and went alliteratively well with 'House'.

I moved into Honeyway House on October 6th 1956. For about a week I felt euphoric. And then the realisation dawned that here I was, in new surroundings, alone as usual, and what was I going to do about it? Whatever answer I devised was bound to be beset with pitfalls. How best would I manage to skate round them? The first pitfalls turned out to be parochial, an area that, unexpectedly, I had not been required to enter until now. I attended, dutifully, a meeting at the rectory to decide upon a new stall to grace the Christmas Fair. Present were three women whom I knew by sight and name and three nondescripts whom I didn't. The object was to decide what sort of stall we would man. All the obvious ones were already annually operating. One of the nondescripts suggested, as though she had had a flash of genius: 'White Elephants' Everybody, happy at not having to give the matter further thought, said what a good idea. Barring myself, who said nothing, as the new girl in the face of unanimity.

Mrs Jones, the rector's wife, rallied me with: 'And what about you, Miss Wyndham?' So I remarked that the term white elephant denoted something that nobody wanted.

After further uninspired discussion, another nondescript suggested brightly: 'What about Connoisseurs' Corner?' This was hailed with relieved acclamation by the majority, but one doubting voice was heard through the tumult to mutter that it sounded very expensive. Mrs Jones, who saw herself as a rallying force, assured us that the rector was a brilliant auctioneer, who had been known to knock down goods hitherto regarded as unsaleable.

At this Mrs de Vere whom I had hitherto regarded as uninter-esting and rather a poseur, and who had not previously spoken, suggested the name Auction Corner and that everything we amassed for the stall should be auctioned. It would be something a little different. For this reason the nondescripts looked intensely disapproving. Impressed by Mrs de Vere's acumen, I said that, for myself, I always tended to get carried away at auctions and to buy much more than I wanted, so that I did think that such a scheme might well boost sales.

Mrs de Vere then turned all the force of her persuasion on me. 'I do think it is a good idea, don't you? I think it will go down well, don't you agree? Will you back me?' I found myself saying that I would, while feeling that it was tactless for any two members to appear to be ganging up against the rest. However the enthusiasm of two served to draw the waverers into a condition of acceptance and, in no time, one of the nondescripts was positive that it would be the easiest thing in the world to obtain from friends and relations a host of attractive pieces for such a sale. I gloomily foresaw no chance of getting anything above the white elephant level.

My next emergence into parochial life was at a tea-party given by a retired cleric, the Rev. Burton, and his wife. Beside myself, the other guests were to be Mrs Jones, the rectors's wife and Mrs Murray, the vet's wife. Mrs Murray, on receiving the invitation, had replied stoutly that nothing would induce her to accept, as she couldn't stand Mrs Jones. Hearing of this state of affairs from Mrs Murray herself, whom I met, by chance, in the town, I begged her to reconsider her decision and to keep me company, and promised that I would telephone Mrs Burton and ask her to issue a second invitation to Mrs Murray. This I did.

Mr and Mrs Murray had been unfailingly kind to me since my appearance in Sussex; he in his advice and attention to all branches of my goats' welfare; she in caring for my dog and cat if I was absent for a night. I admire uncompromising people. They are the only ones whom one is enabled to fully understand, since they will neither prevaricate nor conceal their true feelings, thus ensuring that one is not left with the wrong impression. Mrs Murray was totally uncompromising. If she made enemies by telling people what they did not wish to hear, so be it. Her younger son, Michael, had just begun his career as an actor. At the Murrays house I first beheld the young Maggie Smith.

I was very grateful for Mrs Murray's presence at the tea-party. Mrs Jones and the Burtons, were convinced that to allow the conversation to rise above trivia was to let loose that dangerous explosive, argument. In the face of such a possibility they became visibly worried and upset. Mrs Murray, possibly because she was aware that, in the eyes of the clerics, she came from a lower social stratum, showed off outrageously. While enjoying the show, I had far too much regard for her to let her get away with it. She soon broke through the platitudes to announce: 'I am very interested in music and drama, you know; and I have been privileged to hear all the new tunes from the American musical *My Fair Lady* before it comes to this country. I do advise you all to see it. It is really wonderful. It is taken, you know from *Pygmalion*, by Bernard Shaw. D'you know *Pygmalion*?' We all nodded obediently and Mrs Murray started again, on another tack.

'I am looking forward very much to seeing this new Sound and Light idea Sir Laurence Olivier is doing at Greenwich. It has some wonderful buildings, you know, and Sir Laurence is playing the part of the Duke of Gloucester.'

'Which Duke of Gloucester?' I asked from a genuine desire to know. I could call to mind five of them and, to my knowledge, none had been connected with Greenwich.

Mrs Jones and Mrs Burton sprang, like troubadour knights, to Mrs Murray's defence. 'Miss Wyndham, I do not think that it matters which Duke of Gloucester,' reproved Mrs Burton, chidingly. Mrs Jones chimed in, looking kindly at Mrs Murray: 'At any rate, it isn't the present one.' I said, remorselessly: 'Mrs Murray is telling us things. She should know her facts.' The parsons' ladies looked upset and Mrs Murray, with the utmost good humour, admitted that she had no idea which Duke of Gloucester.

She started off again and when she told us that Sound and Light had started in France, that rang a bell with me and, without thinking, I said 'Oh, of course. *Son et Lumière*.' This must have sounded bad, as though plain English was not good enough for me, but actually it was because there had been quite a long article under that heading in the *Sunday Times* — and I had not bothered to read it.

Mrs Burton and Mrs Jones became more silent and unhappy, but I was now even more interested, and Mrs Murray had one enthralled listener as she related how the history of buildings was told through the medium of light and music. If a child had been born the window of the room in that house was lit up. If the place passed through a bad time it was plunged in darkness. The Rev. Burton wound up the narration by saying that the Duke of Bedford had put on a performance at Woburn and rather stolen Greenwich's thunder. He thus gave away the fact that while he was acquainted with the art form, as it had not happened at Petworth it was not worth discussing.

Loneliness, the dread curse of Graffham, fell away at Petworth, never to return. At Honeyway, without fear or frustration, I experienced the strange, uncanny, unique thrill of love-making uninhibited, and wished to know, and savour, more and more about it. It was a joyful surprise to receive regular visits from William, whom I presumed I had driven away by my neurotic anxieties, pleas and fractious pride. My sole redeeming feature was a willingness to apologise for useless moodiness. To receive the ironic reply: 'I can only presume that I like being bullied.'

Henry Halton was usurping merely the power to disturb me. I met him infrequently during the Fontwell meetings and, more often, during the summer months, at the polo grounds. In my diary I report that:

> He makes me every bit as unhappy as William used to, whom, in disposition, he much resembles. He will be absolute bliss and very attentive one day and ignore me another. He constantly makes promises that he never keeps. He plays on my emotions and keeps me on tenterhooks. And, all the time, I have to pretend to have nothing but the coolest feelings of friendship for him.

He came to tea one day, to see the house. He sat opposite to me across the hearth, Silent, unimpressionable, dull. To rouse him, I asked him how old he was. It did rouse him — to a disadvantaged prevarication. Incensed at the waste of time shared that I had been looking forward to, I pointed out that it was somewhat effeminate for a man to seek to disguise his age. He uncrossed his legs, leaned forward, clasped his hands on his knees and, looking sideways into the fireplace, uttered the ambiguous words: 'Would sixty-five be any good to you?' I did not reply, having received something of a shock. I had supposed that he was barely sixty. The last thing I wanted was a father-figure. I had noted, throughout my life, that while women deduct ten years from their age, men do not reckon to be believed if they drop more than five years. A more definite line would have to be taken.

One Saturday in August 1957 I went to watch the polo. Because it was sunny I took no coat and was perished with cold, sitting up on the stand. Between matches I went to the pony lines, where, somewhat to my surprise I was joined by Henry. I had held him to a promise, made twice in the spring, to show me the foals. He had received me at the Stud, rather grouchily, the previous Wednesday. My view was that, if you make promises, you should keep them and I had come away determined that, from now on, I would insist that Henry honour his piecrust ones. When he said to me, on the polo ground: 'Are you cold? Would you like my overcoat?' I replied: 'Yes, I would,' and stood back to mark the effect.

As I suspected, a bleakness descended. 'Oh, well . . . It's only an old mac. It's in my car. But you could always sit in that. It would keep the wind off you.' Thus was I foiled again. I could hardly take it for granted that Mrs Halton, who looked a most alarming woman, at the best of times, would be enchanted to find a strange, chilly woman cluttering up their car.

8

HIDDEN SHALLOWS

*A*s life improved for me, so I became concerned about my feelings with regard to other people. I wished that I did not feel so repelled by, and find it difficult to be nice to, the dreary, the deaf, the dankly and agedly peculiar. In twenty years or so I might find myself one of them, and need people to be kind to me. I had an old woman, who could claim all the foregoing afflictions, to tea; and spent most of her visit suppressing a mounting irritation. It was five years since I had been abroad. The windows of my mind definitely needed opening. Joan Alexander, now married to Christopher Berry, and I agreed to spend ten days of September at Vicenza. We were not nearly knowledgeable enough to *choose* Vicenza, although our foolish friends told us that it was 'quite a nice little town'. I presume an intelligent clerk at Thomas Cook sent us in this superlative direction. We did have the good sense to read something of the history of the environment prior to our departure.

Air travel has many hazards, but one is spared the mental and physical discomfort of six people cooped up in a small compartment for days and nights together. The tedium induces prattle and that, in all too short a time, is worse than tedium. We shared a couchette with two faceless, harmless, innocuous women, going to Haifa. When we tumbled, cramped and exhausted, out of the train at Vicenza, they were facing yet another night in their bunks, and the dread company of the worst school mistress type, who saw her role in life as that of morale booster and cheerleader. She never drew breath. While the rest of us were helping each other to heave our luggage onto the racks, she sat, inactive, giving out inane advice. The slightest comment that anybody made, she knew better, with long explanations and recollections, she had suddenly called to mind, which would 'tickle us pink'.

Looking forward, as we were, to quite a nice little town, we were thrilled by Vicenza, the gate to such a many-faceted landscape of architecture. While spending a day in Verona, we saw what I took to be a baroque arch. It was Roman. To gain entrance to Palladio's villas in 1957 was as difficult as it is today, and for the same reasons. We were denied the interior of the Rotunda, because the Conte was in residence. We were equally unable to get in to the Villa Emo, because the Contessa was not. She had left for Florence that very day, leaving instructions that nobody should be admitted until her return. This news was broken to us at the closed gates by a charming English girl who, on hearing that we had been looking forward to seeing Veronese's frescos, said 'If it is any comfort to you, I find them very disappointing.'

Of the Villa Vulpe at Maser, the guidebook gushed that the generous owner admitted visitors, neglecting to add, only by appointment. We managed to see the Villa Vulmarani, inside and out, and despised the poor quality of the furniture.

We took the bus to Padua, where we admired the Arena chapel and would have much enjoyed wandering round the city if our demon guidebook had not once more misled us with the injunction that we must on no account miss the Basilique of St. Antony. We walked miles to find it, arriving half dead, to feast our eyes on something that reminded us of the Brighton Pavilion in red brick.

Three times we took the train to Venice and, ignoring the guide book, wandered about at our ease, feasting our eyes and wishing we had three months to spare. One thing puzzled us.

Everywhere we went: in the hotel, in many shop windows, was displayed an English sporting print, *The Meet at Blagdon*. Joan commented at last: 'Obviously the cry goes up, "we must sell the Tintorettos and try and buy *The Meet at Blagdon*,".' We learnt a lot, during those ten days, for future use, about how to do and see when abroad and enjoyed this instructive adventure enormously.

Two days after our return I acted on Mrs Murray's advice and went to London, for the night, to see *Son et Lumiēre* at Greenwich. The friend whom I generally stayed with, and who accompanied me to the performance, had let her flat, so I asked Uncle Hugh Wyndham to put me up for the night in his. He and his wife, my Aunt Maud, had been instrumental in introducing me to Italy, many years before, in the 1930s, when I had been an annual guest at the villa they rented near Florence. In my teens I had lived, during the week, with my grandmother, while I attended a day school in London. During her occasional absences, I had lodged with Uncle Hugh and Aunt Maud at their house in Eccleston Square.

My present visit proved introspectively disturbing. During her final years, Aunt Maud, who had been a very sweet person, with considerable artistic and literary talents, had gradually sunk into a state of near-insensibility, until her recent death. Uncle Hugh who had lost, not only his wife but, like my father, the Petworth inheritance, was not overtly welcoming, and very taciturn. I was allotted, for the night, his deceased wife's bedroom. It was full of her Victorian knick-knacks and the bed was the one, in which I had last seen her, stretched out, as good as dead, and already gone from this world, as far as understanding went.

The whole flat was full of their possessions that reminded me, overwhelmingly, of life as I remembered it in the house in Eccleston Square. The dreary, dark grubbiness of it. The frowsty little study on the ground floor, where we three huddled together round the gas fire. Aunt Maud, with a writing pad on her knees, invariably penning long letters in her large, round sloping, slowly-formed handwriting. Uncle Hugh bent over his desk, muttering under his breath. Always the electric light on. The steep stone staircase, with the print of Lady Hamilton at the first landing. It became a sort of landmark, since there were two more flights to ascend. The walk through sooty Pimlico to school. The walk back again. The deadly sameness of the days. Their mentally infertile dinginess. My total disinclination to learn anything. An unutterable depression overcame me, that it took two days of determination to shake off. Bad though it was, I reflected, to be forty-four, with nothing tangible behind me except the hard learnt knowledge that the lessons of life are the most difficult to profit from; it was undoubtedly worse to be fifteen and dead to all ambition.

On October 7th there was a race meeting at Fontwell Park that I hoped would lead to an opportunity of meeting Henry. While I was watching the sale of a selling plater, I felt my coat being tweaked from behind and heard his voice asking: 'Did you enjoy Italy?'

I was touched that he had remembered, from a passing allusion, made many months before, that I was going there. 'Very much.' I told him, 'but it was disconcerting to discover that Sansovino and Donatello are not just race horses. The original Sansovino was an architect, and Donatello was a sculptor.'

To which this infuriating man replied, teasingly: 'Oh, you are *stupid*. Everybody knows that.' I looked at him, doubting and perplexed. Not for a moment did I believe that *he* did. How could somebody, who never read anything but the Stud Book? He broke the silence to explain that not for nothing had he been dragged round Italy, hating it, by his father. Here was yet another revelation. This Philistine soldier had actually had a father who had been devoted to the study of Renaissance art.

It was a considerable time before I was able to get any further enlightenment on this subject. He was not present at either of the next two Fontwell meetings, the last of the season. His family were there, but as I had not been introduced to them and they had shown no interest in me, I lacked the courage, at that time, to approach them. None the less disappointment and curiosity forced me to take some sort of action. I asked a fellow spinster, who I knew was a friend of the Haltons', to lunch, hoping that she would be able to enlighten me. Fate happened to put out a restraining hand. On the day, the spinster's mother rang up to inform me her daughter was in bed with a streaming cold. Useless to fight Fate. I was prepared to accept defeat. The mother, however, spoke up on her daughter's behalf, suggesting that the disappointment might be mitigated by a later date being set for the lunch engagement. The following Wednesday was agreed upon.

Our mutual friend did not prove worth feeding. Somerset Maughan claimed, in his story, *A Winter Cruise*, that sexual repression makes women over-loquacious. I am not sure that I agree with him, nor on the quieting effect of its gratification, but on Wednesday my guest talked non-stop, so that I despaired of a chance to get my question in. I rushed at the opportunity when she gabbled that she preferred steeplechasing to flat-racing, because she did not bet. 'I seldom do,' I said on instant cue, 'I am usually unlucky, but I have had some good tips from Colonel Halton, so I was disappointed that he was not at either of the last meetings. Where was he?'

She replied abruptly: 'He had a chill last time,' and hastened to resume her own line of thought with such energy that I had no further chance to open my mouth beyond the occasional 'Oh'.

Graffham had taught me the valuable lesson of bearing what one cannot change, changing what one cannot bear, and the wisdom to know the difference. I nerved myself to ring him up at the Stud. The ploy was an encouraging success. We had a stimulating chat and he said I must come over one day and see how the foals had grown. I said: 'Yes, do ask me sometime,' and he said: 'I will, my dear.'

I knew full well it was 'I won't, my dear.' Another piecrust promise. But I was pleased with myself for having shown some resource. Even in these modern days of equal opportunities, many girls baulk at being the first to telephone in a hopeful relationship with a man, although men admit to no aversion from this very safe long-distance approach. If they do not fancy the caller, what more simple than to explain, with deep regret, that they are about to leave the country or are coming down with dysentery.

William's first burst of ardent attention, on my taking up residence at Honeyway, had died down. His visits became as

spasmodic as they had been at Graffham and, although I had
reached the stage of wishing he was Henry, I still missed him, as
agreeable male society, when it was denied me. Waiting for it,
doubting its advent, a chilling sense of disappointment day after
day, called for iron resolution. That I was successful in suppressing
the strong instinct to nag, was proved by the presentation of a
guilty box of chocolates. Fate was not on my side that autumn. I
left the back door ajar, the goats trooped in, found their way
through to the sitting room, prised open the lid of the chocolate
box — and ate every one.

Towards the end of the year I was cheered by an article in
the *Readers' Digest* on the subject of 'How to Manage a Woman',
which stated: 'To get the most from a woman the feeling that she
is needed must be constant, not spasmodic. Men often fail in this
respect, forgetting the constancy of women's emotional demands.'
Demand was perhaps an unfortunate choice of word. But it was
nice to be reassured that my emotions were not neurotic.

Having now seven acres of rough hillside grazing, I increased
my agrarian prospects by buying young calves at Guildford market
and rearing them on goats' milk. At first I sold them, after three
months, for veal. Later I found it a more paying proposition to
keep them for at least eighteen months. Fortunately calves are very
stupid, unindividual animals, so that sending them for slaughter
was not as hard to come to terms with as it might have been.
My brother John, having been instrumental in setting me up in
circumstances in which I could make a life for myself, also, as one
of my trustees, reorganised my finances and, by timely reinvest-
ments, substantially increased my income. He also felt that it was
unfair and hampering that, except with regard to the £300 settlement that my father had laid out for all his children, I had no
power over any of my capital resources. He offered to intercede
with my father to get this financially restrictive clause amended. I
begged him not to. Not only was I determined not to be beholden
to my father for any favours wrested from him against his will,
but I had an instinctive feeling that no good would come of such
an endeavour.

That this instinct was genetically transfused was proved when, some years later, my brother Mark approached our father with the proposal that he should invest in an insurance policy that would increase his income by £400 a year during his lifetime, while lowering the level of death duties that Mark and I would be liable to pay after his death. Our father, as usual not listening, merely answered, with peevish suspicion: 'You are trying to take my money away from me.'

His youngest and least-regarded son retired in confusion. His eldest surviving son, overwhelmed with financial pressures of his own, with the kindest intentions confronted our recalcitrant parent and, with the brashness that the naturally diffident force themselves to assume, addressed him thus: 'You silly old man, can't you see that Mark's idea is not only reasonable, but that it benefits YOU?' My father gave in. In the event he, as usual, was the only person to benefit. For he took his revenge. He made a will leaving his entire estate to my mother. My mother had not made a will. On our parents' death, their children were left to pay death duties at the highest level.

9

THE CONVERSATION OF THE FAITHFUL FLOCK

*A*n amiable couple. Philip and Diana Lamont, had recently come to live in one of the larger houses in Petworth. Mr Jones, the new rector, hastened to exploit them. Mrs Murray told me that Mr Jones was letting it be known that he was disappointed with his new parish. There was this feudal atmosphere. If it meant that he felt he should be experiencing a greater degree of chumminess from his Patron, he, in his turn, treated the ordinary people of Petworth like serfs: ignoring them and never paying pastoral visits. He collected round him a little coterie of the faithful; faithful to Jones first and God second.

My experiences, as a new parishioner in Petworth, confirmed, from thenceforward, my disillusionment with organised religion, indeed the lack of necessity for it. The idea of an Auction Corner stall at the Christmas Fair had metamorphosed into one called Treasure Trove; presumably because the rector feared to put to the test his vaunted talents as an auctioneer. At that year's fair he sidled up to me and breathed into my ear: 'We are having a teaching weekend, with a discussion group at the Lamonts' at eight o'clock on Saturday. Would you care to come?'

I signified my assent, while wondering why the event could

not take place at the rectory, which had a large room for just such an assembly. I said to Pamela at her flower stall: 'The Lamonts are starting mission meetings. Coming along?'

'Not likely,' replied Pamela, 'I don't approve of missions.'

Poor Diana who was less than enchanted at the invasion of her home, cried: 'Oh, do be careful. The rector is just at the back there.'

Pamela stated, with feudal honesty, that she was quite prepared to make known her sentiments to his face. I dropped the joking and tried to persuade Pamela to make an appearance at 8 o'clock on Saturday. Diana turned pale and exclaimed, in horror, that she could not receive the invasion at 8 o'clock, an hour at which she and her family would be approaching the dinner table. She left her stall to seek the rector out and persuade him to postpone his plans until nine.

I was becoming more and more intrigued at the steady emergence of the rector's domineering tactics. The scene took on an even more Joyce Grenfell atmosphere when, on Diana's return, Mrs de Vere stepped forward, with all her conscious social grace. 'Diana dear, I would come and support you, but unfortunately, just that *very* day of course, *everybody* has asked us out for drinks. But I really will *try* and get there, if I possibly can.'

On the night, the Lamonts felt obliged to back up Mr Jones's invitation to me to dine with them. The other guests were the Joneses and the visiting priest, Canon Knight, of St. Paul's Cathedral. He seemed a calm and sensible man. Not that he had much competition. Mrs Jones alarmed me with the news that a party of Evangelists were advancing on pagan Petworth, led by a Miss Gedge, who travelled in an old Ford car, in which she habitually slept, in a sleeping bag. I said that I could not pretend to like the sound of Miss Gedge and her sleeping bag. Mrs Jones assumed her rallying persona. 'I know exactly what you mean, Miss Wyndham,' she assured me. 'I felt exactly as you do, myself — until I found out it is a pink satin sleeping bag.'

When the rest of the group assembled, I was disappointed to note that they were all the rector's trusty lieutenants. None of them was thirsting for knowledge and all had little or no imagination. Mr

Jones introduced Canon Knight and invited the company to ask him questions on any matters that puzzled them. The questions asked were all old chestnuts, such as why does God allow suffering? Mr de Vere wasted at least half an hour by delivering, unasked, a lengthy testimony to his own simple faith; followed, before anybody could stop him, by a further monologue concerning his father's simple faith.

Mr Jones and Mrs Blake, who ran nearly everything that was to be run in Petworth, then settled down to a cross-talk of abuse of his Petworth parishioners. Jones said, would we believe it? that it was almost impossible to get children to Sunday School, because their mothers wanted extra time in bed on Sundays. Mrs Blake chimed in that a woman at Hamper's Green, who wanted to be confirmed, had been scorned and derided by her neighbours. I found the latter impossible to believe and had sympathy with the former who, on weekdays, had to get their husbands up and full of breakfast by 7 o'clock. Circumstances with which Mr Jones had not the slightest connection.

On Monday Canon Knight was to give the last of his lectures at the Town Hall. He had been hard at it, twice a day, since Friday. The subject was to be Christianity and the Situation Today. I felt no great urge to go, but thought perhaps I should help Jones to feel that his efforts on our behalf were appreciated. I took my knitting. After the Canon's lecture, the company split into three groups, under a leader who read out three questions which the group were supposed to discuss until they reached a united conclusion. My group was headed by an old man called Smith, who read the question, expounded his view at great and tedious length and then, if anybody else expressed an opinion, Smith burst in that there was no time to go further into the matter — and proceeded to do exactly the same with the next question. I became very crabbed and, furiously knitting, longed for the guillotine. The next day I met Mrs Murray, who had attended the Friday lecture and had suffered in exactly the same way.

The Joneses were instrumental in teaching me one important lesson in my social development. I invited them to supper to meet Major and Mrs Collins a couple who successfully combined a library/bookshop and a restaurant/teashop under the same roof. For me the evening was a black hole. I enjoyed cooking the meal. Having dished it up, all pleasure fled. The talk, at table, was totally unmemorable, for which I, as hostess, must bear considerable responsibility. Afterwards Mrs Collins and Mrs Jones settled down beside each other, on the sofa, and quacked the evening away with unabated exuberance. I could not hear what they were talking about, because the rector was booming away in my ear his reiterated complaints about his parishioners, punctuated by platitudes on how much better everything had been when he was a boy. All he could keep in mind was the worst side of everybody. He had been a chaplain to the forces. With an equal lack of discretion and compassion, he told of how, during the very heavy fighting round Monte Cassino, he had seen the Guards — 'not conscripts, mind you, Regulars' — go completely to pieces. They had surrendered and were being marched off as prisoners, when a British officer shot the German guard and exhorted them to come back; but they had just walked on, into captivity, as if they had not heard him.

Major Collins filled his pipe and smoked in blessed silence. Reflecting the next day on this dismal evening, I chided myself on not having drawn him into the rector's ungodly recital of human degradation and despair, in an attempt to raise the level of thought and enable the rector to hear another voice than his own. I also noted that, if general conversation is the aim, do not allow two women to sit together.

The retired professional class was as rampant in Petworth as at Graffham, but Petworth House and gardens represented a Disneyland for which they had no entry permit. Mr Jones, who had formerly presided over a well-heeled parish in Cheshire, where he had been accustomed to be the centre of attention, was wont to complain to me also of the feudal atmosphere that, in his view, permeated Petworth. Some of the recent arrivals among his flock were more tolerant and felt that John and Pamela only needed a little kindly advice and guidance regarding provincial standards.

I found myself in the curious guise of pig in the middle. The recipient of cunning advice to hand on to where it was obviously needed. How delightful it would be if my brother were to give tennis parties every weekend, so that this close-knit fraternity could re-enact the pre-war musical comedy opening scene: 'Just between ourselves of course. But wouldn't it be jolly?'

Having taken a wary look at committee women, I shied away from that area too. They were intrinsically jealous of each other: always afraid of being upstaged; quick to relate, with glee, any incident in which one of their colleagues had slipped up. It was amusing to listen to these antagonistic tales from the outside, but there, I reckoned, was the best place to stay. I liked living alone, by and large, although having nobody else's wishes to consider is apt to lead to a set curriculum and self-absorbtion. I dreaded Sunday as a dead day. Edith Evans is quoted as having moaned, on her retirement: 'Every day is Sunday now.'

I formed the habit of asking people to lunch on Sunday, not only to pass the time, but to gain the advantage of hearing other points of view. The supper party taught me that it is a waste of time asking a random choice of available individuals and hoping they will get on together. That way lies boredom and the lowest common denominator of conversation. It is necessary to select intelligent people, with common interests and who are socially aware that the shy need encouragement. It took determination to ask such people to lunch, since inherently I feared that they would not want to come. To this day I will seldom leave a message on an answering machine, because I hear, in my mind's ear, the machine's owner mutter, 'Oh, only her again!' My mother, with no original ideas of her own had, nonetheless, been a skilled promoter of good conversation, by making some remark that sparked off a discussion and working unobtrusively to draw every-body into the conversational net.

Breeding goats and rearing calves, I was involved in the agri-cultural scene and enjoyed the friendship of the farming community. I was, to a certain degree lucky that I had, in rotation, two friends who would put me up for the night in London. Thus theatres and exhibitions were within my orbit. Neither of these friends was intellectually adventurous and they were already, while still in their forties, leading the lives of elderly women. But it was so much easier to stay with one of them than to be forced into making broader plans. I was aware of that unadventurous element at the time, but opted for the easy line. This is such a mistake. To make one's way against the tide of conventional apathy, to determinedly swim past the backwater of the easy commonplace option into the current of competition and wider horizons of mutual intelligent exploration and acceptance of deviations from the static norm, is what I let myself almost miss. I was aware of it because, since the War, I am still refuting any design to fit me into a particular category. Like Groucho Marx I do not want to belong to a club that will have me as a member. There is more laughter to be found outside.

10

. . . . AND OF THE OTHER SORT

*I*t was easy to appear bored at the idea of promoting tennis matches in Disneyland, since I do not play tennis. I kept very quiet about my own forays behind the park wall of Petworth House. Round the dining room table there I heard the best, the swiftest, the cleverest conversational rallies it has ever been my luck to listen to. The table had been made at Chichester in the nineteenth century. It was of mahogany, banded with brass. it had patterned marble inlays at both ends to take hot serving dishes. My grandmother described how the artisans responsible for its construction made a special journey to Petworth to admire their work of art in situ, in a room in which portraits by Van Dyck seemed to be watching the diners. The centre of the table was set with gold cups and candelabra. The company ate off silver plate designed by Paul Lamerie. Very few families, other than royalty, have gold plates. One of the exceptions is Lord Spencer at Althorp.

Round this table friends of John and Pamela, such as Hugh and Antonia Fraser, Ian and Anne Fleming, Peter Quennell, Paddy Leigh Fermor, Lady Diana Cooper, the McEwen brothers, and above all, Judy Montagu, exchanged points of view on every subject, brilliantly. Nobody, in hindsight, seems to have spoken more than a sentence at a time, at which the point would be expanded by somebody else in another sentence, and so on: lightly, wittily, with regular intelligence all round the table. It was too quick and clever for any subject to have survived in the memory all these years.

I think Judy Montagu, the daughter of Venetia Stanley, the beautiful *belle amie* of Mr Asquith, who was shattered when she married Euan Montagu, was painfully aware of her plainness. Her mind was so keen and alert and her nature so kind, that I would not suppose her looks, or lack of them, were nearly so important as she thought them. Her value as a conversationalist far surpassed that of the beautiful Anne Fleming.

Lady Diana Cooper was, of course, a law unto herself, she wanted answers and was quite unmoved if the person questioned was unwilling to give them. Good or bad taste was not a concept in the forefront of her mind. Feeling the same, I was an eager listener and learner. I remember Lady Diana, seated on John's right, interrogating Anne Fleming, seated on his left, concerning some very personal aspect of the love life of one of Anne's children. Lady Diana's voice was curiously harsh for such a feminine type of beauty. She had to raise it to be heard across the wide table. The more Anne Fleming sought to lightly turn the subject, the more insistent Lady Diana became in her leading questions. She did not succeed in getting the full picture, but she got a lot more than Anne wished to reveal. Before the end, the whole table of between twelve and twenty people, was listening.

My brother John was also endearingly open in what he said. I heard him discoursing on the tremendous pleasure of making love, while admitting that it was most exhausting. He had been told that the love act entailed the same expenditure of energy for the male as running up fifty-seven steps. I did not find it exhausting and was most anxious to establish how my partner felt. I found fifty-seven steps — I wish that I could remember where — and ran up them. Whew! It certainly did take it out of one. This knowledge was to add another fear to my already full account. What does one do when one's lover dies on one, in a hotel room, in the middle of the night? Kind friends were only too ready to tell me that it is a not uncommon event, quoting names and gloomy details.

On Monday, November 18th 1957, John and Pamela's younger son, Harry, was christened. Pamela had invited me to lunch, for the event, only the day before. I therefore expected a simple ceremony, attended by my parents and three god-parents. Clearly my brother and sister-in-law intended to have no more children, for I found a glittering finale party assembled. Mr and Mrs Sacheverel Sitwell (godfather), Lord and Lady Hambleden (godfather), Lord and Lady Lloyd (godmother) and Lady Diana Cooper (godmother). Also the Bishop of Chichester with mitre, crozier and all, to perform the ceremony. My mother was so bewitched by the appearance of Lady Diana Cooper that she did nothing but repeat monotonously to anybody who came within her orbit: 'Have you seen Lady Diana Cooper? She is unbelievable. Such beauty. Such imperishable looks.' On my reminding her that, at this stage Lady Diana's looks owed more to art than nature, my mother turned conveniently deaf.

What I found riveting was the stupendous performance that this most distinguished of the godmothers put on. Firstly, her christening gifts were a bell, book and candle: a golden bell, a candle in a gold candlestick and a prayer book, with Harry's monogram, in gold, on the cover and, within, the inscription, in a surprisingly ordinary handwriting: 'Harry's prayer book. The gift of his godmother Diana Cooper.'

She was dressed in an ankle length full-skirted black silk dress, with high-heeled shoes and an astrakhan hat, with a veil over her face, through which the immense blue eyes rolled expressionlessly, assessing her audience. Her hair was goldy-grey, whether true or false it was hard to say. Her skin was flawless, her face utterly unlined. Her mask-like lack of expression occasionally clashed with her gestures: as when she greeted Lord Hambleden by throwing her arms loosely round his neck and putting her face over his shoulder, without a shadow of expression on it. To go into the chapel she put on an extraordinary garment that looked like a mink-trimmed dressing gown. She was to present the baby to the Bishop. A moment before receiving him from Nanny's arms, she flung this garment off with a tremendous gesture and tossed it from her. It was neatly fielded by Pamela's sister, Molly Cranborne. She then took the baby into her arms, with great theatricality, rather spoilt by the fact that she had to pause and ask Nanny, in a stage whisper, what the child's names were.

I was spending that Christmas with Mark and Anne at their home, Langold, near West Malling in Kent. On December 21st I lunched with John and Pamela to receive my presents, a brown leather handbag and a box of Charbonel and Walker chocolates. They told me of R.A.B. Butler's poignant reply when asked what it felt like to lose the Premiership to Harold Macmillan. 'I felt,' explained Mr Butler, 'like a man, who, climbing Mount Everest, makes, after great difficulties, the last base before the summit. He is preparing to make the final ascent, when he feels a tap on his shoulder and a voice saying: 'You are wanted down below.'

I enjoyed my Christmas with Anne and Mark, as much as any thinking person can enjoy that dismal festival, where families are herded together in unaccustomed familiarity and the stock of conversation runs out after the second day at most. I had found pleasure in being taken to dine at Mereworth Castle; which was as good as getting into the Rotunda. I compared with our host, Michael Tree, life before the War and at the present day. He revealed that there was a survival of grand living in Yorkshire, where Lord Feversham, for instance, had not reduced his style of life. While Sir Richard Sykes, of Sledmere, had recently visited Paris and told one of the French nobility, who yield to none in their snobbery, and made the faux pas of asking him what he did: 'Moi, je suis une éspèce de roi.'

John and Pamela had been through a searing time with my parents and our maiden aunt Maggie. My father and Aunt Maggie were now so deaf that every statement had to be bellowed at them individually. On the day after Boxing Day Pamela had sent her maid into their bedrooms to enquire, on her behalf, at what time they wished to leave? This ploy had successfully dislodged Aunt Maggie. My parents were made of sterner stuff and defeated the intention by wilfully misunderstanding. 'Yes please,' they mumbled in turn, 'the same as yesterday. At 8 o'clock. Nothing cooked. And coffee.'

11

BEATING ABOUT
THE BUSH

*T*he year 1958 opened badly. For the first six months I had nobody whom I could leave in charge of my goats and calves, so was tied to Petworth, with no outside diversions. I had what I had hitherto considered a good friend in London, at whose flat I was always welcome for the night. When it suited her, she was in the habit of spending a night or two with me at Honeyway. Now that I was unable to leave home, I begged her to, now and again, come down for the weekend. She had brusquely refused. This was my first experience of a not uncommon neurosis among women who feel that life has given them a raw deal, without reflecting that some flaw in their own personality may be in part responsible. They welcome one's society, are gluttons for sympathy, often have an agreeably wry sense of humour — but, make the mistake of asking for even the smallest outlay of effort in return, and a door is slammed smartly in your face. The fact that, behind that slammed door, their own loneliness is intensified, is outside their capacity to comprehend.

The last time I had stayed with this woman, an old family friend had come to dinner. His brother had, unavailingly, proposed marriage to her, many years before. While our hostess was out of the room, dishing up the meal, my co-guest told me that he had met a man who claimed that it was necessary, for his health and comfort, to sleep with a woman every other night. 'I wonder if he is right,' mused the narrator. 'You and I are the same type: nervous and excitable; what do you think?' My immediate thoughts were that, hitherto, I had had no idea that he was nervous and excitable in temperament; far less that I had ever appeared as nervous and excitable in his presence. I had yet to learn not to be disconcerted by anything that might be said to me.

This is an important lesson for anybody who wishes to get acquainted with the variables in human nature. I replied that it was the greatest mistake to suppose that the emotions of men and women were at all similar. I added, to preclude the notion that I had any association with these animal needs, that I thought that I was inclined to be undersexed.

Afterwards he told our friend that he had found me, on that occasion, good-looking and stimulating in conversation, but that I should do something about my hair. I never stopped trying to do something about it, but no treatment would persuade it to make an agreeable frame for my face. Curiously, neither William nor Henry made any comment about my hair. One was concerned with my sexual education and the other with my stimulating conversation.

As winter turned to spring, the makeshift fencing that I had had erected around the paddock, gave way, on account of the goats' demon propensity for clambering up and bearing it down, with their cloven hooves. A Mr Smallridge appeared, infuriated, at my door, claiming that the goats had totally destroyed his cabbage patch. With due concern, I asked to be taken to view the scene of desecration. There were three rows of cabbages, of which only half a length of one row had been slightly nibbled. Goats are faddy feeders and the common cabbage, when anything better is available, is never one of their favourites.

On February 3rd, my father's sister's husband, General Sir Ivor Maxse, was to be buried, with full military honours, in Fittleworth churchyard. The bearers and trumpeter from the Coldstream Guards missed the train from London, which set the funeral back an hour. 'How very inefficient the British Army has become,' muttered Dame Marjorie Maxse, in the pew beside me. The whole congregation, bar one, was content to sit, like roosting crows, while they awaited the reinforcements. I preferred to walk on Hesworth Common. I came out on top of the Common and sat on a seat overlooking the Downs, which were drenched in sunshine. I thought what a lovely place it was to be — if only I had someone to enjoy it with. And was not that like all my life?

I got back just in time to fall in behind the mourners following the coffin up the aisle. My father and Uncle Hugh were among the number. Uncle Hugh looked three parts dead himself and my father was audibly objecting that the choice of the hymn, O God our Help in Ages Past, was hackneyed. The Last Post, necessarily a very long call, was blown at the graveside by a regimental trumpeter. He started quite pale and steadily turned a deeper and deeper shade of crimson. Uncle Ivor had the distinction of being one of the small number of Europeans who has seen the Indian Ropetrick. Sadly, he was either unable, or unwilling, to give even the most meagre description of it.

From my upbringing I had hitherto supposed that one gets the best results from terrorising the enemy. A child taught me the error of this thinking. A crowd of children from the town used to play, with accompanying shrieks and yells, within sight of my house. It was my custom to rush out at them, witch-like, wielding a broom and screaming at them to clear off. They went; but, within half an hour, they were back. Different tactics were called for. I advanced upon them quietly, in a dignified manner. At sight of me, they fled, all except one boy who, as part of some game they were playing, was lying, face downwards, on the ground. I captured him and said: 'I don't want to be cross. You can play anywhere else in the field, except near my house. It is very annoying to hear continual shrieks and squeals. Do you understand?' Came the disarming answer: 'Yes, Miss Wyndham. That's what my Mum says too.' I was left in peace from then on.

On the 19th February I recorded in my diary:

Lent has started. This year, as well as giving up chocolate, I

am going to try not to think of Self at all. Not to ache for
pleasure and love. Not to fret when things go wrong. It will
be a formidable forty days — and Lent is, I discover, now
I've gone into it, more than forty days. That seems unfair.

The next day I had an electrician in to see to a faulty light in the
kitchen. Twice the telephone rang. Once it was an urgent call to
the electrician, the second time was a wrong number. About five
in the afternoon, it rang again and I answered it rather irritably.
Incredibly it was Henry's voice that said that he would be passing
my door in half an hour. Could he come in and see how I was? I
rushed upstairs and saw, reflected in the glass, a long yellow face,
hung about by lank hair. I did what I could with powder, rouge
and comb and changed into a tidy skirt and silk stockings. I felt
twitchy from the need to appear calm and detached, when I longed
to wind my arms around his shoulders and tell him how very
pleased I was to see him. I had nothing to be twitchy about.

When he came, he sat down and said: 'Now tell me all the
news and scandal.' Leaving, as usual, the conversational onus
on me. I thought that he would be interested in John's recent visit
to India in the train of Harold Macmillan, since all Henry's happ-
iest army reminiscences appeared to be connected with that
country. The Indian authorities had presented to Mr Macmillan
an aged man, stricken with the palsy who, they claimed, had been
thus afflicted since being flogged by the British in the year 1920.

Henry appeared quite unmoved by this and more light-hearted
Indian recollections. I asked if he was pleased at the engagement
of one of his step-daughters. He paused before answering and then
said that he was happy if she was happy; she was the sweetest
thing. This seemed to me unusual phraseology to use about a
daughter. But he had no more to say on the subject. By then I
was down to asking if his other step-daughter's cat had had kittens.
He replied that Joan had two cats, a brother and sister, but that
they were not having kittens.

I remarked: 'How extraordinary.' He asked, mildly: 'Is it
extraordinary? to me it's a relief.' I commented that I simply did
not believe in platonic friendship between cats. He smiled. I had

already noticed that he never laughed. I formed the impression that he was, by nature, vey low key. The impression was erroneous. I never did discover the nature of the bad time he was passing through that year. Its oppression remained memorable by reason of my later discovery that, when happy, nobody laughed more spontaneously.

Now, in a desperate attempt to stir this inanimate soldier into a little liveliness, I embarked on a terrific tirade on the topic of fertility in the village where he lived. Was it a sterile area? Did the leaves come out on the trees? Could it be something in the soil? My companion sat opposite to me, staring at the ceiling, while occasionally glancing at me. To protect his beloved labrador from the rain of aspersions, he volunteered that she had once had eight puppies. That was all. He rose to his feet and prowled about the room, fingering objects and murmuring: 'You have such taste.' He then took his leave. Insensibly, I felt that I had made some impression. But, for myself, I wished that I had retained more impression of what little identity he had shown; had photographed in my mind a mental picture to carry through the days to come. Not for an instant did I query my inexplicable attachment to this uninspiring man.

The next day, Mr Todd, of Graffham, called for my copy of *Country Life*, that I passed on to him and his wife Theresa. I had only got to know the Todds well since leaving Graffham. He was a great exponent of clear thinking. His frequent response to any statement of mine: 'Why do you say that?' kept me on my mental toes. He was known, to his wife and friends, as Toddie. In my mob it was unheard of to call anybody by a diminutive of their surname. The sole exception being the eldest sons of peers above the rank of viscount. In the nursery some had acquired a shortening of their courtesy titles, such as Sunny for Sunderland; Bobo for Bowmont. That was allowable. Toddie for Todd was not. The problem of calling him by his Christian name was that it was Adam, which does not trip easily off the lips. I spent a year or so calling him nothing, before I finally bowed to 'Toddie'.

On this occasion he advised me to read a book, by Hugh Ross Williamson, describing his gradual transition from nonconformity through the Anglican to the Roman Catholic church. Todd found it hard to understand how, after a nonconformist upbringing, Ross Williamson could swallow the miracles of the Roman church. He added the rider that Christianity, itself, was founded on the most extraordinary miracle of all.

I replied: 'I cannot accept that miracle, any more than you can, but I can accept miracles of visions and healing. After all, even if you cannot prove their veracity, neither can you disprove it.'

Todd said he considered that science disproved it, to which I countered that science could only prove matter. Was it not admitted that very little was yet known about the mind? Visions emanated from the mind.

Todd asked why, if I was prepared to accept some miracles, I was unable to believe the original one? I pointed out that birth was not to do with the mind. It was an essential functional phenomenon. And you couldn't monkey about with that.

'Oh, can't you,' laughed Todd. 'What about AID?' I said that that was the same principle; merely a different means. Did Todd seriously mean to infer that AID was a step in the direction of virgin birth? Todd rose to take his departure. 'The door is ajar,' were his last words on the subject of our discussion.

While we were talking, I was reflecting in one corner of my mind that, while I found Todd more congenial, keener-witted, of greater interest than Henry, why should he, nonetheless, leave me cold, while the ostensibly stupid cavalryman caused me to ache with love for him?

I wrote in my diary that I thought it was nice of God to send me Henry as a bonus and that I could not really feel depressed after such a pleasant thing had happened to me. But I was haunted by longing for him and the fear that I had either bullied or bored him while he was with me. 'Longing, in fact,' I added, 'for certainty and security. Two things that are never for me.'

I daresay such feelings are preferable to the ones that I would surely feel now, of irritation at having wasted my time and attention trying to please somebody so tediously and ungratefully unresponsive. Appreciation should never have to be a one-way street.

During the next month he called once or twice for short visits. My tirade would appear to have fixed cats in his recollection, as he told me: 'That cat of ours is behaving disgracefully now with three other cats.'

'What about the little white one, her brother?'

'Oh, he sleeps with her at night, but he gets his chums in to help during the day time.'

A certain amount of enlightenment was granted me at the Point-to-Point meeting. Before it, I lunched with John and Pamela and heard the story of General Montgomery approaching Sir Winston Churchill to break the news to him that his old regiment was to be amalgamated with another. The embarrassment of the responsibility was increased for Montgomery by Sir Winston constantly interrupting the carefully prepared statement. 'You are not trying to tell me that they are doing away with the mounted band of the Household Cavalry?'

'. . . No, no. Nothing like that . . .'

'I hope the King's Troop of the Royal Horse Artillery is still intact?'

'Yes, of course. It's about the 4th Hussars that I've come to see you.'

A great sigh of relief. 'Oh, *that's* all right. It's my funeral that I am worried about.'

An incident with a similar background had occurred to me a few days before at Fontwell. It was raining. Approaching the stand for the first race, I stopped to talk to the Hunt fieldmaster, Johnny Moore, who was standing on the lower steps, in the open. A voice higher up, speaking from beneath the shelter of the roof, said: 'Ursula, come and stand up here, out of the rain.' It was a command, not an invitation. I left Johnny and obediently joined Colonel Halton. His wife was standing beside him, but I appeared to be invisible to her. A Clever Wife does not treat a potential Other Woman as invisible. Astute acknowledgement is one of the many cards with which wives can, almost invariably, trump a rival's ace.

Addressing Mrs Halton's husband I said: 'I read in the paper that two squadrons of the Life Guards are being sent to Aden to relieve one squadron of the 13th/18th Hussars. Am I to understand that one squadron of the 13th/18th is equal in efficiency to two squadrons of the Life Guards? Because, as daughter of an old colonel who commanded the Life Guards, that does rather make me bristle.'

To which Mrs Halton's husband replied: 'As an old colonel who commanded the 13th/18th, that is right.' Although Mrs Halton's first husband had also been a 13th/18th Hussar, she appeared to be deaf, as well as blind.

Henry acted as starter to the point to point. I saw him in the paddock, with the starter's flag tucked under his arm. We had quite a crack on the subject of combining forces to go to Guildford market to buy calves. I saw a man photographing us, who then aproached and announced that he was from the *Queen*. 'I know you are Colonel Halton,' he said, 'but may I have this lady's name?'

Shortly afterwards Henry, in altered tones, said hurriedly: 'I'll ring you about Guildford.' For the first time I saw Mrs Halton standing quite close. She was looking at me rather fixedly, but not glaring, as she usually did. I was a little taken aback and murmured that I must go and look at the horses. I made no effort to speak to him again, but feeling some concern lest I had stayed at his side too long, I stood at the entrance to the paddock when the horses were leaving it for the last race. Henry on his horse, followed them. I did not catch his eye, but heard him say: 'And how is Miss Wyndham doing?'

I answered quietly: 'I am not doing anything, in fact.'

He turned in his saddle, as he passed me, and said: 'It's very difficult,' and gave a confederate's wink.

12

COMING TO GRIPS

*I*n May I drove over to look at Wilton House, near Salisbury. I was entranced by the house and its setting and the two Cube Rooms, with their heavy gilded decoration; so different from the rococo of the White and Gold Room at Petworth, but exactly suited to the older and more castle-like aspect of Wilton. The party of tourists, of which I was a member, were under the guidance of a man whose easy mastery of the subject and an intolerance of questions, made me almost certain that this must be David Herbert, a son of the house.

In a corridor, he paused at a print of Covent Garden, explained that it also had been created by Inigo Jones and indicated that, if any of us chose to go there — he clearly had not been, himself — we would find it totally unchanged since the time that it was built. This was more than I could stomach from Mr Herbert. I spoke up: 'There is only one quarter left of Inigo Jones's arcades.' Mr Herbert, with the languid certainty of one who knows, and is not accustomed to being contradicted, informed me that I was mistaken. I turned to the crowd: 'Come on,' I said, 'do none of you know Covent Garden?'

A small man at the back put up his hand as though we were

in a class. 'I live there,' he told us. 'I don't recognise any part of the print.' We were silently hustled on to the next item of interest.

On the 19th of May, a month after the Point-to-Point meeting, I went to watch the polo. There were few people there. I heard a fellow member, in the stand, tell her companion: 'Everybody is at Windsor, and Henry is ill.' I depended, in vain, on the companion to ask the necessary questions. All she said was: 'At least the X-rays were clear.' The ladies made so little of the indisposition that it was impossible to be alarmed.

When the photograph appeared in the *Queen* I cut it out and brought it to William's attention. He, also was in a disenchanted mood that month. 'That old rogue,' he commented. 'Well, at least you seem to be enjoying yourself.'

I chose to go to the polo on Saturday, May 31st, instead of Sunday, because it was a fine day and tomorrow's forecast threatened rain. I met Henry who said: 'It is ages since I've seen you. Not since we were photographed.' We spoke momentarily of horses, and then Joan came along with his dog. At the beginning of the second match I entered the enclosure just behind him. He stood in the background and was soon surrounded by a group of people. I chose a chair to sit on that had another just beside it. I reflected that he had not appeared anxious to retain my company. Life had been very dull lately. The desolation of feeling that I meant nothing to him descended on me. That I must swallow and submerge in the endless daily round my love for him. I looked round and he was looking at me. But, at that distance, he might be looking in my direction, at some other object. More time passed. Now he was out of sight. Then, suddenly, there he was beside me, taking the empty chair. He was attentive, beguiling, enchanting. I fell in with his mood and responded to it. For half an hour, until the match ended, we sat together in blissful teasing chat.

It was during this period that I had a telephone call from William that he wished to come at once to my house and make love to me. This is not the sort of precise intention that a respectable matron is accustomed to receive. I had not the slightest desire to make love with him. But . . . we had been through a great deal together; experiences that were woven into the fabric of both our lives. Who was I to refuse him, who had seldom refused me?

I have never been an exponent of the point of view that the hearthrug is as good a place as any for an erotic encounter. When William arrived, I took him upstairs with all the formality of a chambermaid or housekeeper preceding a guest. Uncomfortably aware of this, I put on a performance of ecstatic excitement which I have every reason to suppose he thought was genuine.

I had not felt any sense of guilt with regard to William's wife. They led their own lives. I was not *in* love with him, nor he with me. I was neither stealing nor trespassing. Since my heightened awareness of Mrs Halton at the Point-to-Point and on the stand at Fontwell, I had given some thought to her existence in the background. In her husband's life it was in that situation that she was always to be seen. She was seldom at his side in public. She did not appear to mix with his friends. Some of his polo companions considered her disagreeable and a heavy drinker. He assured me that she did not mean to be unfriendly. She was very, very shy.

It seemed to me incongruous that a woman who had had two husbands and reared three children and was now in her fifties, should retain the nervousness of an inexperienced schoolgirl. I, with far less experience of the world than Mrs Halton, had forced myself to overcome my shyness. It behoved me to attempt to discover what kept her so cripplingly inhibited that she relied on alcohol to give her Dutch courage.

My study of Mrs Halton yielded very little fruit. She repulsed all my conversational approaches as, seemingly, an unwarranted encroachment on her privacy. I knew that her one great passion was hunting. She no longer rode, but she followed the Cowdray Hounds, by car, every day that they hunted, and spent time at their kennels. Her only friends were women who were equally obsessed. Only on the subject of hunting, did I get a very slight response. My efforts had no success other than that, when we met, she achieved the pitch of exchanging the time of day with me, in the flat voice of couldn't-care-less, before passing on her way.

That her husband felt an unyielding sense of guilt concerning her I was to learn, and the knowledge kept her always in the forefront of my mind. Over the next sixteen years I was to arrive at the conclusion that, at some point in their relationship, he had subjected her to more than she had been able to take. Like the women whom I have already mentioned, she had retired, fatally, within herself: unwilling to experience any further emotion, whether of pleasure or pain, concern for others, or any other motive beyond the purely routine. I felt that, in becoming Henry's mistress and helping him to satisfy his wife's material needs, since he had not been, for years, a sharer of her sexual ones, I could, by restoring his sense of fun, lighten and make warmer their relationship.

The path of love does not only not run smooth. Worse; it does not necessarily run true at the start — a stage at which a Romantic would hope that it did. The first deterrent was that I contracted ringworm from my calves. Sensibly, I thought, I asked Mr Murray, the vet, to treat my ringworm at the same time as he did that of the calves. The result was that, although the calves responded well to the treatment, my arm became itchy, considerably inflamed, and the ringworm worse.

I rang Mr Murray, who advised me to consult my doctor, as the trouble was clearly due to his animal lotions being too strong for my skin. I must, on no account, let the doctor know that Mr Murray had been treating the condition. I said that I saw no possibility of keeping the news from him, as my arm was stained blue from the lotion. I was primed with the statement that the vet had left the lotion with me and that I had used it on myself, on my own initiative. 'This could land me in prison,' claimed Mr Murray dramatically. 'I would come and visit you,' I promised soothingly. 'Hopefully bringing a cake with a file inside,' was the final veterinary advice.

Henry had found Rowse's book, *The Later Churchills* on his last visit and proclaimed that Sarah, Duchess of Marlborough had a very long neck. I replied that I had never noticed this in any of her portraits and then, light dawning, had added: 'I think you mean Consuelo.' It appeared that, to him, one Duchess of Marlborough was synonymous with any other. On his next visit,

I put the book, open at a picture of Duchess Consuelo, in his hands.

'There is your long-necked duchess,' I said.

He placed his fingers round my neck and said: 'Like this long-necked duchess,' which satisfactorily confirmed my original supposition that it was my neck that he had in mind.

'I know why you admire her,' I went on, 'it is because she looks like a racehorse.' He neither confirmed nor denied the simile, but took the book from me and, turning the pages, made comments on other members of the Churchill family. I was sitting very close to him. Fearing that he might think it a deliberate invitation, I moved a little further away. At once his arm came out and encircled me, while his other hand fondled my breasts. I was conscious of two over-riding thoughts: How depressingly like William's his approach was — like plodding along an only too well-known road; and that a continual procession of people were walking along the bridle path at the top of the rise and, if I could see them, the chances were that they, through the wide French window, could see us.

I felt a purely inquisitive wish to kiss him. He was nuzzling his face into my long neck, but displayed no intention of seeking my lips. I found his mouth, but again there was no enchantment — nothing at all. I was now concerned that my encircling arms would bring him into contact with the ringworm. I voiced both these fears. As I think he found me just as uninspiring as I found him, he let me go with great good nature. I rose and said: 'I think I had better go back to the armchair.'

Conversation, as always after this sort of nonsense, was very difficult to get started againt. Once begun, we went on very amicably and enjoyably. The mutual appreciation that we had so utterly failed to find in physical contact, returned in the exchange of ideas. At parting a vague plan was made that some time I must come and look at fencing at the Stud, as I was still having trouble with my boundaries. He was away from home for the next two days. During that time I felt warm and comfortable about our relationship.

Looking forward, the well-known road now, in anticipation,

offered fresh and unexplored vistas. He had commented that he liked to do with people he liked what they liked. I had not questioned this potentially wide spectrum, since I suspected it to be a narrow one. But the spirit showed a willingness to please.

I met him at the Stud on the day after his return. He asked if he might accompany me back home. When I gladly acquiesced, he explained that he had first to get out of a previous engagement, to visit a sick friend. I listened, my mind pervaded by a warning of possible personal experiences ahead, while he dialled a number and spoke suavely into the receiver. 'Hello, Peter. Look, it's such a fine evening that I think I must stay and get some work done. Can I come in tomorrow?..Oh dear. Well Thursday then.' I wondered whether Peter had been fooled. It sounded very thin to me.

When we entered my sitting room, he clasped me joyfully in his arms. And, in doing so, dumped me back on the well-trodden road. He wanted to be reassured that I liked being man-handled. While giving the assurances obediently, the wider side of my mind reflected, is one always to go on repeating this, like a parrot? Has he no sensitivity to responses? In the present instance the demonstration was a prelude to discover whether I was prepared to go further. But the invitation, it appeared, was supposed to come from me. In this respect, my hero was Young Lochinvar. And should be. No wonder that man has become a legend. I intimated that I was prepared to do what he liked. So we went upstairs, out of view of the pedestrians.

What came to light was that he was completely out of practice. After twelve years of marriage, it appeared that I was the first invader. He was admirably self-possessed, charmingly and concernedly apologetic, took all the blame. His sang froid, lack of humiliation or dismay were utterly endearing. The more so since I had formed the opinion, later to be amply justified, that much of what imagination he had was focussed on women: their desirability and the emotions that the sight and thought of them evoked. The only thing that put me out of step was that, in an area where I looked for leadership, I was to be obliged to take the initiative.

How deeply this was at odds with my character I was to come face to face with at our next encounter.

At the next meeting he took me in his arms again. This time I thought I knew my lines, and suggested that we go upstairs. He was very surprised, but acquiesced. I would have given anything for the strength of mind to cancel the invitation. In my bedroom I endeavoured to engage him in harmless conversation. He threw me on the bed, with the words: 'I'd no idea you were this kind of woman.' I was filled with extreme self-revulsion, combined with anger. I reviled him; then, my spirit breaking, I confessed: 'I feel awful and terribly ashamed. I don't want to be thought a loose woman. You, yourself, suggested it yesterday. You come into my house and mess me about in full view of the populace.'

Holding me close, he said: 'I know. It is my fault and I *like* loose women. But I am not up to being raced upstairs at a moment's notice. I need time. What I'd like is a nice quiet night with you. You say you go to London for fun. Well, so do I . . .' I made it plain that I did not at all go along with such a brazen plan. He kept me there, warm in his arms, consoling, teasing, rallying, comforting, for half an hour or more. 'You have quite well-shaped breasts,' he said, fishing one out, 'but they are too small.'

'It is only because I am lying flat,' I felt it necessary to explain, still heavily on the defensive.

He went on: 'And you've got a nice little bottom.' This condescension was intolerable.

'That,' I stated, 'is what Mellors said to Lady Chatterley. Yesterday I was a long-necked duchess. Today I'm a gamekeeper's moll.'

'Do you like me at all?' he asked, very earnestly. We seemed to be acting in a very bad play, in which he was stealing all my lines. Now that he had pinched this one, the cue had to be handled with the greatest care. After due reflexion, I responded with: 'I have wanted to fold my arms around you for the last three years.'

'Have you really?' he said, in accents of surprise, but he gave no indication as to whether he was pleased or not.

A month or two later, when he asked me: 'Did you know

that I would fall in love with you?' I felt safe enough to confess that I had loved him, to distraction, for three years.

'Why didn't you *tell* me?' with typical male astonishment when confronted with what, to the female, is obvious.

'Because,' I told him gently, 'if I had, you would have felt that I was chasing you. You'd have run like a hare.' He acknowledged that possibility.

I reported to my diary the next day:

> I am still terribly sore in spirit and hurt and slept very badly. I think it is very good for me: I am so bad at bearing pain. I have resolutely forced myself to work diligently and to uncomplainingly accept the ache. And, in particular to be kind to everybody and not to hit back if people seem, in any way, tiresome and offensive to me.

13

JUDY O'GRADY AT BLENHEIM

Suffering can be found in the most unexpected places. Pamela, motoring to London, stopped at a red light on the Kingston by-pass. In her rear mirror she saw a car approaching at such a pace that it was clear that it could not pull up in time. With great foresight, she let her brake off to lessen the impact, when it came. She helped to pull the unconscious driver, covered with blood, out of the wreckage of his car. An ambulance arrived within minutes, but the breakdown van broke down on its way to the scene and a second breakdown van had to remove the first breakdown van, before starting on the cars. Pamela was not anxious to leave her car before help arrived, as her jewel case was wedged in the smashed boot. An endless procession of kindly people approached her with the invitation: 'Mother says won't you come in for a cup of tea.'

Thinking it churlish to refuse all these offers, she followed a man back to his house. She was ushered into a kitchen where a curious scene stood revealed. The television was blaring at full strength. A weeping woman was hard at work at an ironing board, while a surly youth was packing kit into a knapsack in one corner. Pamela's escort, to whom she had clearly come as a boon and a blessing, said: 'Don't mind Mother; she's a bit upset because our boy's joining the Navy.'

Pamela, in the light of this information, naturally thought the hearty approach was the right one. 'That's splendid,' she enthused, 'such a wonderful opportunity to see the world. My father was in the Navy and he loved every minute of it.' The woman let out an anguished shriek and moaned: 'All those foreign girls!'

Pamela, still doing her best, veered round and proclaimed: 'It's all right. We've got no foreign ports now. He'll always be in home waters.'

The youth stopped packing and looked at Pamela with deep dislike. There was triumph in his voice as he reminded everybody: 'There's still Singapore.'

What I had to learn was what the young man packing his knapsack was so keenly looking forward to: freedom from domestic and family fetters, and a spirit of adventure. Henry wanted me to share every aspect of his life. He was also jealous of my own pursuits, to the touching extent of expressing an interest in ancient architecture. This I eradicated, once and for all, by taking him to Westminster Abbey. The orderly old soldier was horrified. He looked, askance, at the untidy melange of statuary, memorial tablets, tombs. How dare the authorities permit such careless chaos? Half the stuff should be cleared away and the rest arranged in neat rows. I feared that he might write an admonitory letter to the Bishop of London.

The telephone rang every day and his voice issued the order: Prepare to receive cavalry. There were to be moments in the future when I was wont to remind myself, ruefully, that this means that the enemy is about to charge. My sixteen years service as Judy O'Grady had begun. The role of Judy demands a rather too full stretch of acting ability from someone suffering, *au fond*, from a sense of inadequacy. The Colonel looked on me as his concubine. The dictionary definition of that is secondary wife. The fact that his wife at home went nowhere with him, made my presence at his side less flagrant. Few of his friends asked after her; all accepted my presence pleasantly and without comment.

I had, nonetheless, to accustom myself to a certain amount of invisibility. This I encouraged, often walking ahead when friends hailed my colonel to talk to him at race meetings. I felt no sisterhood with the colonel's lady, but I was determined that I would not, under any provocation, be the cause of her suffering. It was a climate that I was sufficiently acquainted with personally, to wish vehemently not to visit it on others. If this philosophy sounds complacent, that was a word that I would have given anything to have even a nodding acquaintance with. Lacking it, I had to formulate my rules as I went along, accepting that my one certainty was uncertainty: every plan was subject to unforeseen cancellation.

The first experience of the elaborate fencing stances that are a necessary protection when two people progress under false colours arose when, having proposed to spend my birthday with me, Henry later made it known that he had received an invitation from his old friend, Sir Algernon Peyton, to stay with him near Bicester, the night before my birthday, to discuss farming matters. He had not yet accepted the invitation, pending a discussion with me. I told him to go.

He suggested that I should accompany him and stay with my Uncle Humphrey and Aunt Ruth, who lived close by. I said that was indeed a good idea, if I could think of an excuse. A wish to see Blenheim should prove sufficient. Henry said he would like to see it with me. On my claiming that such an expedition would bore him, he embarked on a discourse of the sights of Florence, to prove his passionate interest. I suggested that, should Blenheim not be open on Saturday, it might be as well to give it a miss and just pick him up. After all, it was only an excuse and not part of an important plan. I would think up something to tell Aunt Ruth. As I had expected, he showed obvious relief. Both of us had reckoned without my aunt.

When I rang her up, she was most welcoming and showed no surprise at my sudden whim not to be able to exist any longer without seeing Blenheim Palace. The fact that it would not be open on either of the days that I would be in Oxfordshire appeared only to fill my aunt with an enthusiastic determination to enter into a battle of wits with the Duchess of Marlborough, to force an entry into her home.

We set out on this expedition of September 19th in glorious weather. We stopped at the Complete Angler at Marlow for lunch. Walking in the garden, Henry professed a knowledge of roses. 'Horses and roses are your joint interests,' I suggested.

'And women,' he added, taking my arm. Passionately interested he certainly was. Duchesses and molls: he loved them without distinction. He had less knowledge of the workings of a woman's mind than any man I ever met. It had caused him to make two disastrous marriages, without any increase to his understanding. I realised early on that I must get to understand him, because he would remain unable to understand me. I was only the second woman in the long list of his loves who had bothered to understand him. The first one he still remembered with passionate intensity after twenty years.

We watched the river sluicing over the weir, and then we went and took our places in the dining room. The menu revealed that the cheapest meal available cost twenty-one shillings. I, who had accustomed myself to thrifty living, exclaimed: 'I never heard of such robbery. Don't stand for it. Let's go.'

We did, Henry remarking, during our exit, that he had never been bounced out of a restaurant by a woman in his life; and that I reminded him of his Aunt Edith, of whom he had been terrified as a child. I asked him had he then wanted to pay that much for a simple midday meal? To which he owned that no, he certainly had not. We lunched, less luxuriously, but very adequately, at the George and Dragon, on the opposite side of the river. Afterwards, still delightfully en rapport, we strolled down Marlow's attractive main street and he bought me some chocolate truffles.

Upon arrival, I thought it was well to make known to my aunt and uncle that I had travelled with a companion, in case they heard of it from the Peytons and because a telephone call might be necessary, on either side, in order to synchronise our departure. My uncle, being my father's brother, accepted the information without interest. My aunt flustered me by making too much of it. How very extraordinary. How had we known that we were both coming to the area? And on the same day? She had already been in touch with the duchess, who had not refused, but made use of the evasive tactic to ring her up the next day to remind her.

On Saturday the news was that Her Grace had gone out and would not be back until lunch time. At lunch time my aunt met with a very frosty response that would have put a lesser woman off. We arrived before the noble façade of the Palace at 2.15, to be told that the ducal party was still at luncheon. We drove up to the monument in the park, and back to the house, which was an admirable opportunity to take note of the surroundings which were the remains of the old Plantagenet hunting park of Woodstock. The party were still at lunch on our return. From there my aunt took matters into her own hands. We entered by the private side entrance, crept past the dining room and toured the state rooms. As we emerged from this escapade, we encountered the duchess. She was every inch a duchess: handsome, haughty and anything but friendly. My aunt by contrast was tall, jolly and quite unsnubbable. She succeeded in causing a thaw in the coldness.

Aunt Ruth suggested we should pick up Henry on the way back, to save time. I was instinctively against the plan. Two considerations inclined me to favour it. Firstly that I feared Henry might be getting impatient. Secondly that Aunt Ruth would have an opportunity to note the difference in our ages, which I hoped would rid her mind of any incipient suspicions. She was a constant receiver of my mother's 'What's the news?' telephone calls. Henry appeared a little embarrassed by the unforeseen invasion. My aunt and his host stood chatting interminably, while we shifted from one foot to the other. These two things put me out of my stride, made me mervous, when we drove away at last. Also, he had forgotten that today was my birthday. Two days before he had presented me with a bag full of gifts, with orders not to open them until the day.

One of two characteristics that separated him from the common herd of mankind, was that he gave presents in bulk, thus creating the excited expectation of a Christmas stocking. The other — which I consider even more important — is that he seldom used the conventional, unthinking, prototype endearment of darling. My Precious, Lovebird, Angelheart, was the more imaginative music that fell upon my ears.

The birthday presents had been a baby bottle of chianti, a bottle of Omy bath essence and a bottle of Balmain's Jolie Madame scent. Also *Bowhani Junction*, by John Masters. This was in deference to the alarming fact that I read books. I looked at *Bowhani Junction* with some derision. An adventure story, set in India. How typical of him. But why should he imagine that it could possibly interest me? None the less I kindly read it and made the important discovery that it was a first rate story, skilfully written by an author of undoubted distinction. From his father, Henry had inherited a natural good taste; even concerning things that he did not know much about. He also wrote to Hatchard's second-hand book department for Banjo Paterson's *The Man from Snowy River*, an Australian classic that nobody's bookshelf should be without.

Passing Brookwood cemetery, on our way back from Oxfordshire, the trees to be seen behind the high wall prompted me to quote Christina Rossetti.

> When I am dead, my dearest,
> Sing no sad songs for me.
> Plant thou no rosebush at my head,
> Nor sober cypress tree

The poem made no impression on him. It was not the Song of Solomon. 'Do you,' he asked, 'know a lot of poetry? Have you a retentive memory?'

I replied 'Yes, But such a tiresome sort of retentive memory. I can remember poems, dates, telephone and car numbers, but not what I am doing the day after tomorrow.'

'But what's the point of remembering anything so far ahead? Why not keep a book and write it down?'

Because it is so tiresome having to write everything down. And isn't always successful. You scribble memoranda over everything. Yet when I see the intriguing note: 'Creel's nose?' and ask what it means, your usual reply is: 'I don't know.'

He took my hand, raised it to his lips, and said: '*I can* tell you the answer to that, and I will if you like; and then, perhaps, we can let this subject drop.'

I said: 'Well, I felt cornered. When I'm cornered, I always fight to the death. I'm sorry. You'll just have to say "shut up!" '

When we got home he said 'I think my family are away tomorrow. Would you come to lunch?'

The next morning he rang up to say: 'I am afraid there can be nothing doing today. Plans have changed.' This is a concubine's lot and I accepted it philosophically. He asked if I had anything to tell him? To which I replied that, if I had I would only remember after I had put the receiver down. He said that he would be at the Stud for some time, so I could, if I wished, ring him back. In those early days he habitually went to the Stud on Sundays in order to call me.

Upon reflection, I realised that as I had expected to have my main, midday, meal out, there was virtually no food in the house. I rang Pamela and asked if I could lunch with her and John on account of the unexpected situation. I then rang Henry to tell him that his refusal to feed me meant that I was facing starvation. He was suitably distressed. 'I have managed things,' I reassured him. 'I rang up Pamela and told her what you had done and she said it served me right for putting my trust in a full colonel. With my experience of them, I should have known better.'

'I hope she didn't say that,' he said — as usual not knowing when to believe me and when not.

The lunch with my brother and sister-in-law was enjoyable. After it, we drove to the top of the Downs in beautiful weather and picked out all the local landmarks, with the aid of binoculars. Pamela saw the Brighton Pavilion, quite clearly, in a spot where it could not possibly be.

14

VERSIONS OF FIDELITY

*H*e persuaded me to spend a night with him in London, the success of which had the not unexpected effect of heightening and increasing our feelings for each other, to a degree that both found it difficult to control. Our individual methods of coping with this passion were mutually antagonistic. I focussed on the fact that he was so much older than myself. He, that I was a humble goatherd, whom he had had the kindness to pick out of a ditch.

He and his wife were due to stay with her cousin, which was their annual holiday. He complained that he was tired and in need of the break. Truly concerned for him, but also over-anxious to prove the emotional freedom of my objectivity, I pointed out that coming six miles out of his way every evening, to see me, must materially add to his fatigue and that, on this account, I was prepared to forego the pleasure of seeing him daily. He was instantly suspicious concerning the purity of my motives.

'That is very self-sacrificing of you,' he observed, in a noncommittal voice. 'Shall we then not meet before I go?'

'Oh yes. I hope you'll come to say goodbye.'

'That is very melodramatic of you.'

I said, laughing, that I enjoyed being melodramatic — and so did he. I instanced the distinctly erotic expression he could invest in the single word 'Goodbye'. How, in telling me the telephone number of the Cavalry Club, he had made it sound like an incantation: Gros — ve — nor 1 — 2 — 6 — 1.

'Oh yes,' said Henry, as if he minded, 'you were very mocking about that; when all I meant was that you should not mishear me over the telephone.' I thought that he was being absurdly pompous, and said nothing. This gave him the opportunity to use his own weapons.

'We must find a husband for you. I should like to watch you going up the aisle.' I could have cried out from the pain, but forced myself to a recollection of the surprises and raptures connected with our night in London. I got a ready response. At the back of my mind I was bandaging my wounds with the decision to use Johnny Moore, at next Monday's Fontwell meeting, to note Henry's reaction to another man monopolising me.

Johnny Moore was kindly, friendly, amusing, responsive: just the man for the job I had in mind for him. We had two sessions of laughter and badinage that Monday. I do not know whether Henry witnessed the first. I had the satisfaction of noting his eyes fixed on us during the second. In the stand, later, I found myself beside Mrs Halton who, to my surprise, actually greeted me and asked me how I was. She then left me and I watched her weave her way through the crowd milling between the stands and the rails. Arrived at her goal, I noticed, for the first time, that it was her husband. He was standing with his back to the rails, facing the stand. Across twenty yards of crowded space, his eyes met mine. He snapped his jaws. I raised my head in acknowledgement of the gesture, and smiled down my nose.

The night in London and the Johnny Moore technique yielded rich fruit. I was a lovely adorable woman; I amused him and made him laugh; and — in tones of half-embarrassed awe — I made him feel *so* much younger. I recognised that the laughter and the restored sexual vigour were my strength. On a less conscious level, I came to terms with the fact that, for him, a most important outlet was that he now had a whipping girl. It would upset the delicate marital equilibrium at home to scold his wife or argue any decision of hers. The pent-up resentment could be released on me. 'I never dare argue with you.' (I, who loved and depended on understanding through discussion and debate). 'I felt sorry for you: this poor lone woman, who had nobody but goats.' 'I think it is good for you to see me.'

Mostly, I took it as the price a concubine has to pay. If it kept the home front peaceful, it was a worthwhile service to perform. If I did demur, the 'wonderful, unbelievable, adorable woman whom he couldn't believe his luck to have found' record was displaced. Therefore, I got to distrust mere words. To rely on instinct, sensitivity: whether the mutual feeling was right between us. If it was not, what resource to draw upon to restore it?

All *he* wanted to know was how many men I had slept with. Jealousy has never been one of my many problems. With him, it amounted to something near to mania. His relationship with his wife had probably snapped because he became jealous of an old mutal friend. He forbade her to see him on a specific occasion. She, conscious of her innocence, and wholly ignorant of emotions she had not personally experienced, paid no attention to the order. I can only too well imagine the fury of his reaction and her failure to come to terms with the, to her, unaccountable fact that she had lost him through no understandable fault of her own.

'What does it matter,' I asked, 'how many men I have been to bed with? All you have to hold on to is that I am a one-man woman. I don't ask you how many women you have gone to bed with. If they made you happy, I love them for it. I have not, by the way, been to bed with what you call Bloody Moore.'

Language must have come late in anthropological evolution. Presumably that is why human beings still find it woefully inadequate in mental understanding, and why two witnesses seldom give the same account of one event. Henry's jealousy was primeval. Not long after we became lovers Jack James telephoned and invited himself for the weekend. It did not enter my head that anybody could be jealous of Jack. He was not attractive, he was neurotically egocentric, I did not even like him very much. He could be good company for a short time. I told Henry, who appeared absurdly suspicious but, on receipt of the foregoing information, expressed himself satisfied; other than that it was a very odd thing to do: to have a man to stay for the weekend. This was years before I learnt of his wife's fatal slip.

Jack was due to arrive in time for lunch on Saturday. At about 11.30 Henry entered my house, unheralded, to announce that he could not endure it and, that being so, there was nothing for it; we must part. Totally at sea, I asked why? Because this man was coming to stay. I ought to have known it was too much to ask of him. I pointed out that in order to guess that I would have to have had some degree of tenderness for Jack. I felt nothing more than if a brother was coming to stay. If he had confided his feelings in time I would not have hesitated to put Jack off. Now it was too late; he had started on his journey. I drew off my finger a ring that my grandmother had given me. I said: 'Take this and whenever you feel distressed, clasp it very tight in the palm of your hand and realise that it is a token that I can never be false to you and will never have a man to stay again.'

If I supposed that from henceforth giving my lover no grounds for jealousy would be simple, I was wrong. While I was milking a goat, it nuzzled my neck. I got no impression of being bitten. Therefore, when Henry questioned me, in a furious voice: 'Who has been biting your neck?' I was sincerely puzzled. The more I denied any such encounter, the angrier and more unreasonable he became. There was a mark on the side of my neck, a bite; and he knew a man's bite if anybody did, so that it was useless to deny it. The goat incident then returned to my memory, but at this late hour, was treated as another fabrication. It was not till, thoroughly frightened and despairing, I burst into tears, that he accepted this age-old feminine refuge, surprisingly, as the truth.

'Very well,' he said, 'I believe you. And now we will not mention the matter again.' I was expected to leap back, from fear and anguish, to being once more his laughing teasing concubine.

It cannot, then, have been on this occasion that he revealed to me his original astonishment that I was prone to rock with laughter when we made love: 'I thought it little short of mad at first.'

'Did all your other women submit to you in dead silence then?'

'Oh, they did a little cooing, but not your gales of laughter.'

'But how else can I show you how much I am enjoying your attentions?'

'Yes, I realise now that that is what it means and I like it, but it surprised me at first.'

He never ceased to surprise me. He was very susceptible to the catharsis of drama. We went together to the film *Gigi*. To my slight embarrassment, he wept openly and unashamedly; especially while Maurice Chevalier sang 'Thank Heaven for Little Girls.' He told me how deeply moved he'd been by a film that he had once seen, about a couple in love, who were torn apart by circumstances and conflicting loyalties. Predictably he could remember neither the name, nor who had acted in it. During his continuing description I identified the film as *Brief Encounter*. I said: 'I think the woman probably would have gone off with the man . . . Except, I don't know; she had quite a nice husband, hadn't she?' He said simply: 'You know, it is very difficult to get away.'

He was apt to revert annoyingly to the subject of why he had picked me up. I did not remind him that the boot had, in fact, been on the other foot. I intrigued him, he would say, invariably adding, in justification, that he had felt sorry for me. 'Now I find,' he appended on one occasion, 'that you were really perfectly happy: that you liked goatkeeping and you already had a man.' This set me thinking. The inference was that to have a man, however unsatisfactory, was better than nothing. Would he have rushed to the rescue if I had had a drunken husband? Why does aloneness seem to some people the worse fate? Is it?

I had quarrelled with William during the summer, because he professed to be too busy to help me with my fencing problems. He dropped in one evening in November. I was pleasant, but not chummy. I could see by his expression that he wanted me to be chummy, but also that he was reluctant to climb down. I was in the immensely strong position, that I had never been in before, of not caring whether he did or not. He told me, and told it well, a lot of amusing gossip. He stood by his car, prior to departing, looking at me with his immensely expressive eyes. It was like dipping into a well-remembered and once favourite book: one could interpret each page at a glance. He got into the car and said: 'So you wouldn't take my hay.'

I replied: 'After the way you treated me in the summer, I don't wish to take anything more from you.'

'With regard to the fault there, it was six of one and half-a-dozen of the other. When I am in a temper and overworked I don't mind what I say.'

'Well I do. I have never been spoken to as you did and I am not going to risk it again.'

He said brusquely: 'Well, I apologise.'

I said: 'Very well.'

He said: 'D'you forgive me?'

I gave him my hand, which he raised to his lips, and I said: 'I'll try to. I've been feeling very bitter about it. But you've done me an awful lot of good and I don't forget that.'

He said: 'And you to me.'

I leant forward and said: 'Give me your cheek,' but it was his lips that I got. I felt very humbly proud that I did seem to be able to keep the affection of men, once I had gained it. He came once more for a chat. When he went, the recollection of all, good and bad, that had gone before, caused me to say instinctively: 'Come again.'

He knew women far better than Henry did. He looked at me intently and said: 'Do you mean that?'

I uttered the one word, 'No'. I never saw him again.

15

THE TRIBULATIONS OF A CONCUBINE

*F*rom thenceforward I was free to devote my whole being to the vocation of forging a perceptive and reciprocated commitment to a totally loving relationship. The fact that our ethical values differed so radically helped to make our long-term connection one of continuing psychological discovery. Boredom, the bugbear of all human relationships, and the initial reason for most acts of infidelity, was a state of mind we never knew after the early stages. In the area of patience and understanding it is harder to be a concubine than a wife, if only because few men realise that. The excitement of stolen meetings, the word-play to cajole and agree upon the best means of achieving this aim; above all the on-going discovery of new facets of the beloved's personality, in the constant need to adjust and re-arrange, precludes any aspect of boredom. Surprise is of the essence.

Although Henry's eyes would fill with tears at any story of a woman's fortitude in her relations with a man, by contrast he was intensely nervous of unhappiness openly displayed by a woman. I received the order that I must never cry, because his wife often did. I noted with surprise and an emotion that I was not permitted to reveal, that any trait practised by what he described as 'a wonderful woman', must never be seen in me. Nor in any other woman.

He commented adversely on the conduct of a Mrs C. She was, he stated, a most disagreeable woman. She came to the polo, with a bad-tempered look on her face, determined not to enjoy herself. She sat by herself, apart from other people. She could not be troubled to speak to anybody. Tears of frustration and perplexity gathered, unbidden, in my eyes, as I replied: 'How can you mean that? You have given an exact description of your wife.'

There was a moment's startled silence. It seemed long to me; I was holding my breath. Then he said, in tones of wonder: 'I'd never thought of it in that light . . .' His voice died away, uncertainly, before he consciously rallied. 'But she is not like that at home,' he assured me — or was it himself whom he was reassuring?

I said: 'Neither is Mrs C., I expect.' I longed to ask questions, to probe this extraordinary mystery. I could not. It was as if an iron curtain had descended between us.

It rose, only to descend again at unforeseen intervals. As when he said to me, in the High Street at Newmarket, a propos of what I cannot now remember: 'Perhaps if you ate more you would not have these aberrations.' I made no reply, telling myself complacently that I could soon get even on that one. The opportunity, that a clever woman would have passed over, came as I drove him to Bedford to spend that night. 'I wish,' he informed me, 'that you would not drive so close to the kerb. My wife does it, and the other day it nearly caused an accident.'

'I wish,' I announced, 'that you would not muddle me up with your wife. We are two totally different women. Perhaps if you ate more you would not have these aberrations.' He made no reply, but there was no triumph for me. The curtain came down, bringing with it a freezing atmosphere that pervaded the whole evening, the night and the next morning, when he dropped me at my door. The early part of the night had passed in a recitation of his wife's virtues: she never got upset and when, long before, his first wife had made him so unhappy, by her unreasonable behaviour, that he had got drunk, his second wife, then married to a brother officer, had put him to bed. The former virtue did, indeed, seem one to be coveted; the second struck me as par for most courses. What else could she have done with him? He made condescending love to me in the silence that I maintained. At the time I was pathetically grateful. Later I hated myself for such servitude.

He kept away from my door for a week, although he rang up every day and wrote letters signed with all his love. I pulled myself together, kept up my spirits, was agreeable on the telephone and played the waiting game that my past experience had taught me and that needed more long-term discipline than I had, in fact, got. The weather was very hot. I longed to be taken to the private beach at Angmering to bathe. I was informed that he was too busy: an excuse that I knew to be false. In one of these calls he revealed that he was acompanying his wife on a short visit to her elder married daughter. 'It will give them pleasure,' he explained, adding: 'I have always felt it to be one's aim in life to try and make people happy.' I heard myself dealing out praise and agreement for a humane sentiment. Upon replacing the receiver I felt sick with the sense of complacent falseness that I had helped to generate. Waiting for telephone calls was equal to the dependent misery so brilliantly and shamefully portrayed in the prose of Dorothy Parker. Next time the telephone rang, I got in first.

'Who are you intending to make happy today?' I enquired objectively.

'I must look at my list,' replied that maddening, beautifully modulated voice. 'I think I have got down to the Ws.'

'Really. I know of nobody whose name begins with W whom you have ever been in the habit of making happy.'

He laughed, and exclaimed: 'You are awful!' followed by the news that he had a few things to see to and then he would come over and we would do whatever I liked. So we went to the sea, that day and again the day after. It was delicious and he was in his nicest mood. Lying on the sands in the sunshine it was easy to make the unrancorous statement that I had suffered a lot of unkindness during the last fortnight. Guilt was subconsciously acknowledged in his instant reply of: 'Nonsense!' He was sure that he had said nothing unkind: certainly hadn't meant to, followed by the infuriating insinuation that I had doubtless had the curse, which always made women unreasonable.

I remarked, idly, while letting sand drizzle through my fingers, that it was odd that what he said to me was not supposed to be nasty, yet when I said exactly the same to him, it was. He laughed, wholeheartedly and admitted sheepishly that my riposte had enraged him at the time.

On the third day, trying, like a good Libran, to be fair to everyone and keep the balance even, he took his family to the sea. The following morning he rang up in low spirits. 'Did you enjoy yourself?' I asked.

'Quite,' he replied. As he had plainly enjoyed himself very much with me, this was music in my ears. It was followed by one of the occasional outbursts that punctuated the whole of our relationship, and that always took me by surprise and shook me.

'Oh God!' he groaned, 'we sat in the exact spot that you and I did. I could have cried.'

If we saw our respective positions and the whole subject of ethics from an opposite point of view, that remained a constant area to be explored in the orbit of mutual responses. I realised that he lied to me upon occasions. I told myself that, as long as I was aware of this weakness, it was not important. It was a relief to arrive at the discovery that he was not, in fact, a natural deceiver. He lied from fear of the consequences of telling the truth and was edgy from the subsequent fear of being found out. When I had taught him that, in my eyes, the role of the Other Woman gave me no valid claim to him, I was trusted henceforth with the true aspect of his problems.

This climate made our commitment fuller, stronger and firmer. Plants need rain as well as sunshine. He wished to introduce me into his home. Joan's cat had had kittens again. At Fontwell he approached me with his wife in tow. He said, as though she spoke no English: 'Enid asks me to ask you if you know of anybody who would take one of Joan's kittens?' I addressed myself to Mrs Halton with questions as to age, sex, colour, etc.

Henry then intervened to suggest: 'I think that Ursula should come and see them, don't you?' Mrs Halton maintained a mutinous

silence, such as a truly shy woman would have been too embarrassed to persist in, in view of the fact that she had asked a favour
that would involve considerable enquiries and trouble. Out on the
racecourse for the three mile steeplechase, he and I found ourselves
alone.

'You must not ask me to your home,' I protested.

'Why not?' he wanted to know. 'I thought it was such a good
opportunity, but you would not back me up.'

'If Mrs Halton was nice to me,' I pointed out, 'I could not
continue to be your mistress.'

This was not a point of view he had heard from either of
his wives, both of whom were living. Neither had shown any
consideration for the other. Neither appeared to be happy and
fulfilled women. Their tactics, therefore, were best avoided.

On our expeditions to London it was very difficult to find
accommodation, and, when found, it was not precisely what one
would expect. Twice, as a last resort, we went to a hotel near
Marble Arch. We used it on two occasions, lacking any alternative.
The first time we were allotted a room containing five single beds,
arousing wild speculations as to what species of traveller the hotel
was accustomed to cater for. The shape of the room and the
dispersal of the beds made it impossible to tie two together. Henry
fell out of the one that we crammed ourselves into, at a stage when
the proceedings were about to become really interesting. I found
this more amusing than he did.

On the second visit there were only three beds in our room.
While we were unpacking, Henry handed me a book *The Unfair
Sex* that he had borrowed from Joan, which, he assured me, I
would find very amusing. It was unfortunate that I should chance
to open it at a chapter headed 'Don't Have An Affair With A
Married Man.' I read:

> The most unsatisfactory lover in the world is the man who has
> a wife. A liaison with him is encumbered with all the
> inconveniences of a love affair, plus the irritation of having a
> rival who outranks you. In every aspect of your relationship
> with him you feel her influence. The very hours you spend
> with him are dictated by her tastes, her schedule. Whatever

her habits, you must at all times be prepared for the sudden
cancellation of a carefully planned rendez-vous and equally
be prepared for the unexpected message that he is free, just
when it is least convenient to you.

I turned on him furiously: 'I don't think this at all funny. It is
entirely true. I know it only too well. What a thing to give to me!'

'But darling, you're not supposed to take it seriously. You
laugh at it. Joan thought it very funny.'

'Joan is very lucky indeed that she *can* think it funny. There
will probably come a time in her life when she can't.'

He took me in his arms and confessed: 'Oh dear, I've done
the wrong thing. I thought I'd amuse you.'

'You are a fool, Henry. It is much too near the knuckle.'

I spoke with a lightness of tone that I was far from feeling.
Useless to upset him when he had meant well.

We went our separate ways: he to the Cavalry Club, I to shop
before visiting an old aunt. When I returned he was in the bath;
still very concerned and loving and appeasing, so that I began to
feel ashamed at having raised my voice. I drove him to his dinner
at the Grocers' Hall in the City, before prudently dining, myself,
with two female friends. The next morning I resolutely picked up
The Unfair Sex and began to read it. I was soon laughing heartily,
as it was indeed very funny. I had my revenge by reading aloud
from the chapter headed 'The Married Man', discovering, as I did
so, that he did not find it amusing from the opposite angle either.
'Listen to this', I cried broadmindedly.

> When you do get together, your married beau, with
> commendable caution, will rule out all the nice places to
> which you ask to be taken, and you will pass the time tucked
> away in some little room or in your own apartment. This has
> the value of being economical as well as discreet — an important
> consideration for a family man.

Henry objected crossly: 'You can't call *this* a little room.'

I continued blithely:

> In any event, the fact that a man takes a sweetheart does not
> indicate that he prefers the sweetheart to his wife. Ninety

times out of a hundred he would be aghast at the idea of trading
his good old wife for a wanton stranger.

I was able to raise a chuckle of broadminded laughter. Henry gave
a very dim smile. He was, however, pleased that I had learnt to
laugh at the book. On the way home he said: 'I did like watching
you kneeling on the bed, in your little nightdress, laughing away.'

To avoid the difficulty of finding civilised hotel accommodation, we formed the habit of going to the Park Lane Hotel in
Piccadilly. It was expensive, but it had advantages: a garage for
the car, in which my dog could sleep, and it was close to the
Cavalry Club, where Henry was supposed to be staying, and
where he could look in, after breakfast, to see if there were any
messages from home. This meant that I descended, later, from our
bedroom, alone. The one-armed liftman never failed to say, with
a leer, 'How is the gentleman this morning?' It left the impression
that I might have been pleasuring a different gentleman on each
occasion and was one of the many such insults to which the
concubine has to become accustomed.

The liftman had an excuse to take an immoderate interest.
The foyer of the hotel was the waiting ground of obvious, but
often rather elderly, prostitutes: painted and bedizened to make a
somewhat pathetic sisterhood. They fascinated my gentleman, who
would pause, entranced, to look them over, when he should have
been entering the lift with me. There were times when I had to
leave the lift, before its imminent ascent, and haul him in.

It was the first mini skirt era. In those days they were shift-
like garments, devoid of decoration, other than the faint protuber-
ance of the buttocks behind and the bosom in front. Viewing
the young females progressing along the pavement, thus nubilely
arrayed, Henry lamented that he had not been born twenty years
later. Out of the four hundred beds in the Park Lane hotel we
were amazed to be told that only twenty of them were doubles.
As regulars, we were kindly treated by the management. If the
hotel was full, they would accommodate us in one of the suites,
at no extra charge.

It took me years to accept the hotel scene. I felt a personal sense of squalor that loving should have to take place, in secret, in a place reeking of illicit relationships. The whores were a welcome cathartic element to turn the situation into a self-mocking sick humour. Henry pointed out to me a hotel in which a friend of his was wont to hire a room for a few hours in which to sport with his mistress. Not only did I express the strongest disapprobation of this style of jollity, I refused to consider that hotel even for an overnight rendezvous.

At the end of seven years, on reflecting that I no longer felt such reservations, other than concerning a by-the-hour booking, I was equally shocked to have to admit in myself such acquired nonchalance and loss of innocence.

16

THE MILITARY MAN
CONSIDERS LOVE

*H*enry's overwhelming interest in sexual practices coupled with a keen recollection of those women who had particularly taken his fancy, in turn fascinated me, since it was such a distinctive part of his character and an aspect of which he had learnt to be ashamed. He was wont to refer to 'my unfortunate desires' and a dictum that had a firm place in his philosophy was that the rampant cock knows no conscience. If he believed that, why was his sense of guilt, though unexpressed, so tangible?

I took all these things and pondered them in my heart.

His wife had enjoyed the sexual act, but had brought to it her social attitude that it was getting that counted. Giving should not be expected of her. She would make demands of people and their property, as of right, which were sometimes embarrassing. One such, that I heard of in the planning stage, I begged Henry to exert himself to prevent, because of the unfavourable gossip that it would undoubtedly promote. My intercession disturbed him so much that he rose and left the room. I followed him, still pleading. With his back turned to me, he addressed the wall: 'You don't understand. If I ever had anything out with her things could never be the same again.'

It was like a closed door suddenly swinging wide.

After five years of marriage, twelve years before we met, he had ceased having sexual intercourse with her and wished to move into the spare room. The idea of nocturnal separateness had upset her so much that he continued to share her bed to sleep in. It seemed, to my way of thinking, a fatal decision. Far happier to meet afresh each morning with a kiss. Communication with Henry needed, above all, to be tactile. What he referred to, in time-honoured fashion, as John Thomas was at the same time a part of him, yet having a separate individuality: a sort of beloved twin brother, inseparable, yet distinct. John Thomas's sensitivity was acute, the vulnerable side of Henry's ego, to be loved and cossetted by me as part of our mutual bonding and the system by which we operated. Some bygone whore had instructed John Thomas in a highly exciting technique, that included an almost complete with-drawal, leaving the woman on the brink of feeling unconsolable loss which, as she became aware of it, was succeeded by a deep tremendous thrust of unsurpassable gratification.

It is useless to attempt to pick the threads of an intricate relationship, but this organic dualism, involving so many facets of the female psyche's responses, made for a lasting commitment and a strong sense of oneness.

A French prostitute, named Emilienne, lived in his memory, since, when she was stricken with tuberculosis, the whole of his regiment had contributed to pay for her medical treatment, which, alas, proved ineffectual. During World War I he had made an assignation to meet Emilienne at St Omer. She was to approach St Omer by train from Paris; Henry rode twenty-five miles on his charger to reach the rendezvous. Upon arrival, both participants made the discovery that St Omer was a closed area. Emilienne was not allowed to leave the train; Henry rode the twenty-five miles back to camp. His comrades-in-arms thought it a huge joke.

The woman to whose memory he remained the most faithful was Marylee from Instowe in Devon. They seem to have shared a strong instinct for sexual freedom, since, annually, they made a point of celebrating Independance Day together. The 1939 War separated them, as it did so many other friends, but he kept, in a locked drawer, all the memorabilia concerning her. It was clear that he wished, with hindsight, that he had married her. They had shared a complete affinity of interests and opinions and, in her, he had found a warmth of heart that his spirit desperately needed. He had tried, unavailingly, to persuade the owners of the Stud to name one of their foals 'Marylee'. I registered two white kids as 'Marylee' and 'Emilienne'. Marylee became my most successful show goat. Emilienne, by contrast, was second-rate in every respect. I was sorry about that, since the original Emilienne had provided perhaps the more sympathetic story of the two.

A third love of whom Henry spoke was the only one that I met. I cannot remember her name. She suffered from the defect of being personally unmemorable, although her full-length photograph, as a young woman, depicted a slim well-proportioned girl of undoubted appeal. But she was a simpleton. She loved him too obviously and in vain, a circumstance that he found not a little reassuring. The time came when she trotted out the time-worn threat: 'What would you say if I were to tell you that I am thinking of marrying So-and-so?' Perhaps she was taken aback to receive hearty congratulations. At any rate, she married So-and-so and continued the affair with Henry. During her husband's absence she became pregnant and Henry paid for the abortion that she was unwilling to have.

'I think that it was the right thing to do, don't you?' he said to me. I had to reply that, for myself, I could detect no element of honesty and rightness in the entire narrative. This easy attitude to problems: that you can pay your way out of them, is the philosophy of unthinking youth. Henry may have argued that it was not his fault that he was irresistibly attractive to women, whether he wanted them or not. He definitely considered that it was the husband's responsibility to keep his wife faithful to him, but, if he failed, the responsibility that passed to Henry was not to allow a worthless woman to foist on her husband another man's child.

She came to stay, by now an elderly woman, with a friend in

the neighbourhood. In Mrs Halton's absence, he asked the old chum round for a drink, with several others, including myself. Joan acted as hostess. I had been most anxious to meet this character out of his past — and correspondingly disappointed to be presented to a little, dumpy housekeeper of a woman, full of merry clichés. There was no remaining trace of the pleasing female figure of the photograph in the old bundle at the drinks party. To Henry she remained the woman who had loved him. When he returned from escorting her to the door on her departure, he said, after doubtless quite a few drinks: 'Well, well, to think that I once nearly married her! But there it is, one has to be in love to marry,' I had some difficulty in restraining the observation that evidence was still wanting that he had been in love with either of the women he had married. Joan civilly filled the breach by asking me to stay to supper. I have always regretted that, in the light of so many mixed emotions, I refused the invitation.

In the very early days there had been a Mrs Grant, whose husband had been a major in the regiment of which Henry was a subaltern. He had had her on the floor of his father's house in Upper Brook Street. We made a pilgrimage to the house, which is now offices. We pushed open the front door and turned left to enter the room in question, which was empty. This circumstance enabled Henry to point out to me the exact spot where the loveless exercise had taken place. On another such occasion, at regimental headquarters, Major Grant had tactlessly interrupted them. All he could find to say had been: 'Hi! I say. She is *my* wife.' To which Henry, standing, as soon as he could extricate himself, to attention, had replied: 'That is undeniable, Sir.'

That, with the passing years, he learnt a sense of responsibility for his actions and, with it, a recurrent, uncomfortable shame is the most likely explanation for my failure to achieve complete understanding of the miserable relationship with his second wife. She had been, like Mrs Grant, the wife of a brother officer, but in this case the husband had been Henry's friend. She had been sympathetic and understanding over his despair concerning the spitefulness of his unloved first wife. As always, with Henry, emotional involvement could have only one end. When Mrs

Halton's first husband was killed in World War II, Henry's achieved sense of responsibility felt the onus of his old friend's widow and children. She was not the type of woman to make friends easily, still less one whom men lusted after. This, in Henry's mind, was a cardinal point in her favour: to settle down, with an attractive, ready-made family and a grateful wife and to say goodbye to the demon of jealousy was, recollecting his past, more important than the sensual element that had always proved fatal. That it might not be enough for her, he, of course, had never thought to consider.

Expiation is a very uncomfortable companion. It cannot, in fairness, be expressed without belittling the person who has caused it and making something of a saint of the expiator. Servicemen are trained not to sing their own praises. Hence that final closed door that I tried, in vain, to force. At the same time my openness, the fact that my experience of life had taught me to think of the plight of others and my teaching that, in fully understanding, it is easy to forgive, was what kept his love for me constant. That, and the strategy of playing ultimately into his hands in the area of discussion. The male ego is a frail plant that it can be a woman's pleasure to nurture.

This passion for sexual adventure and for female admiration that, however much he got of it, he was never previously to take seriously nor believe to be permanently his, was endearing and so much a part of him that it was only natural to wish to understand it and to teach him that he could trust my undeviating devotion and my interest in any person who interested him; but never to dare to take me for granted. His mother had been a superb Edwardian beauty. I have a photograph of her, gazing out upon the world with an expression of total self-confidence from beneath a huge hat, enshrouded with ostrich plumes. His dedicated businessman of a father had lost his money in some City disaster. His wife faced up to this emergency by taking a lover called Willy Isaacs. Henry spoke of her as of an unknown distant goddess.

Each of her four sons had two wives, following a first failed marriage. The family was Roman Catholic by conversion, having fallen under the spell of Cardinal Newman. I was introduced to and became friends with Henry's youngest brother, Joseph, and his wife. Words like 'adultery', 'living in sin' or any oblique reference to sexual licence filled them with such obviously acute embarrassment that Henry, who had, perhaps, had to face more facts than they, took a wicked pleasure in teasing them on the subject.

There was a more lewd side to his fantasies that he insisted on sharing with me. He sent for parcels of pornographic photographs that arrived in plain wrappers. His erroneous supposition that I would find them equally fascinating — a truth that I kept from him — was only transcended by the realisation that I was expected to harbour these unwelcome volumes. When I pointed out to him that they would make a far worse impression in a spinster's dustbin than in his own, he was unable to appreciate the situation from any other point of view than that it was unthinkable that his wife should be made aware that he sent for such packages. Why, I asked, should she mind when he took it for granted that I would not? I got no answer and the incriminating evidence was left in my hands.

In this predicament I rang up my nearest male neighbour and explained my plight. Within five minutes he was on my doorstep in a condition of pleasurable interest. Yes, he could certainly remove the pictures. The chaps at the factory where he worked would be delighted to see them. He would be a popular figure. 'Before you take them to the factory,' I suggested, 'do let your wife see them.' He thought I was insane. Of course he could not think of showing this kind of thing to his wife. Yet he had not been in the least surprised or considered it unfitting that they had been shown to me. I was relieved to have it confirmed that Henry had apparently only behaved like any average man, but it remains an aspect of average men that I can never hope to understand.

From Henry I heard of all the varieties of the male insatiable search for sexual excitement, including voyeurism, which seemed, to me, the most inexplicable. My experiences at the hands of my parents had left me with the natural wish to follow the opposite road from the one they had dragged me along behind them. One of these alternative directions has been a decision not to sit in judgement on people. Nothing that he told me shocked me and the element of sordidness was entirely redeemed by the fact that, when immediately after we had made love together, he lay with his eyes closed, on his face was an expression that I can only describe as one of noble ecstasy. I kept my eyes focussed on this expression in wonderment. I was incapable of achieving this height of transcendency. Excitement, delicious frissons, yes. But not the peak of human sensation that brought that word 'noble' into my mind.

This was uncannily close to mysticism.

17
WORDS FOR MISCONCEPTION

*I*t is a small wonder if I retained an innocence with regard to certain of my lover's instincts; I was eqally unaware of my own. I knew that I had no maternal instinct: I had no interest in dolls and cuddly toys as a child. It came, therefore, as a shock to discover that I had a strong reproductive instinct and that the two are unrelated. For me a strong part of the excitement of lovemaking was that it might make me pregnant: a sort of Russian roulette in reverse. Instinctively I felt that the act of sexual intercourse was only the first step to a long involvement the right true end of which resulted in birth nine months later. I did not waste these details on Henry. I merely epitomised them in the information that, being in love with him, I wished to bear his child.

'I don't think that would be a good idea,' he objected. 'I can see you walking along the edge of the polo ground with a baby in your arms, pointing at the umpire and saying, in your piercing voice: "Look, there's daddy." '

I was a little taken aback that someone who did not know the first thing about me, should conjure up an all too likely picture. I explained that I had no intention of keeping the child about me until it could look after itself. I presumed that it would still be possible to farm a baby out, as many mothers who could afford to pay for this service had been accustomed to do since time immemorial. My enthusiasm caught an echo in his ego. He presented me with a small booklet enumerating a wide choice of girls' and boys' names. We fixed on Katina for a girl and Guilbert for a boy, because, within two months of the start of our liaison, I, who was unfailingly regular, had missed a period. By the time that I had missed a second our hopes would have been high, but for one baffling circumstance: I was not being subject to bouts of sickness. I was feeling particularly well. I lacked the bravado to ask for a medical test.

Hitherto it had been I whose nerves had been stretched the most with regard to the difficulties and uncertainties of spending as much time as possible together. At this momentous event in our love affair it was he who reiterated: 'I must be able to see you more often.' Highly charged human relationships all too often illustrate the buckets-in-a-well syndrome. Occasional is the joy when both buckets are at the same level. Henry devised, as he did everything, with the attention to detail of a military exercise, a romantic scheme by which we could enjoy a week together in the South of France, at Cannes. He was one who made life-long friendships, whereas I tended to outgrow what had appeared to be kindred minds which, after a time, became static.

At his prep school had been a French boy called Pierre Poignard. They had never lost touch. Poignard was now the manager of a golf club near Cannes. Henry could ostensibly be staying with this dear old friend. From the Hotel Mediterranée, overlooking the old harbour at Cannes, where he and I booked a room, he could make daily telephone calls to ensure that no message had been received from home and been ignored. Monsieur, being French, would naturally be sympathetic to anything involving an *affaire du coêur*.

About ten days before we were due to embark on this adventure I began to suffer slight haemorrhages every three or four days, lasting no more than an hour or two. As the day of our departure approached, the condition worsened. I felt not only let down, but rather a fool. So this was why I had experienced no morning sickness. How idiotically presumptuous to suppose that I was pregnant. Instead it was clearly an early warning of the bodily disturbance heralding the menopause. I rang my doctor who was only too happy to confirm my diagnosis and advised a medical examination. I explained my holiday plans and asked if he could give me anything to avert the bleeding for a week. On my return I would submit myself to his diagnosis and advice. He gave me a medicament to close the mouth of the womb. This precautionary measure worked well for a few days.

It was my first visit to the fabled Côte d'Azure. I was unpretentiously delighted by the whole scene. Our bedroom overlooking the sea and Cap d'Antibes, the square where Napoleon had assembled the first legions of his loyal troops on his return from Elba; the three corniches giving access to La Turbie, Roquebrune, Cap d'Ail, as well as Nice and Monte Carlo. The Casino, with its weird old harridans, covered in jewelry and covetous for sudden riches. Henry, while anxious for my pleasure was less happy. The bucket that was myself was high with a sense of freedom in that, for a week, Mrs Halton's demands were off my back. The bucket that was he was low from the knowledge of living a lie and the unforeseen aspects of the revenge that Fate might take.

We went to lunch with the Poignards, whose presence had made this truant holiday possible. Monsieur Poignard was markedly lacking in Gallic charm. There was none of that insouciance associated with Maurice Chevalier and Charles Boyer. He was formal and unsmiling and he addressed me persistently as Madame. In view of the French connotations of the word I took this ill. His second wife, Yvonne, was a brassy blonde of limited intelligence, but at least she was friendly in the form of making giggling her means of communication.

After three days the mouth of my womb unfortunately opened once more; at first only with the spasmodic symptoms that I had experienced at home. Before the end of the week, while having a cup of coffee on the terrace of the Carlton Hotel, I experienced a terrifyingly embarrassing haemorrhage. All hopes of every sort appeared to be wrecked. I was no longer a loved woman, a fertile woman, a woman enjoying a winter holiday in the sun. In one fell minute I had become a social and physical leper, entirely on my own.

Seats on a plane were swiftly booked. In London I bade farewell to Henry and told him that I would get in touch only after I had coped with the present crisis. I telephoned my doctor who arranged for me to consult a gynaecologist at Guildford. I rang the woman who was taking care of my goats and asked her to bring my car to Guildford station. I spent most of the journey to Guildford sitting on the lavatory seat.

Jilly Cooper once reported in the Press the shockingly insensitive treatment that she endured at the hands of a gynaecologist when her pregnancy continued to develop only in the Fallopian tube. I was glad to have this knowledge, since, without it, it would have been even harder than ever to endure the shocking inhumanity of a professional medical robot to a woman in a state of distress that probed the very depths of her biological feelings and emotions.

The man into whose consulting room I was shown was tall, of gross build, with small mean little eyes and a completely bald head. He seemed aware that he looked like a monster and had carefully acquired a manner to match. He diagnosed fibroids with complete conviction. He said that he was due to go on holiday that week, but would pass my case to a colleague with the suggestion that he should remove my womb. 'On account of fibroids?' I queried. Not precisely for the fibroids, he informed me. At my time of life menopausal symptoms would equally cause floodings, so that a hysterectomy would satisfactorily dispose of all these transitory embarrassments. I stated that I did not want to lose my womb. 'It is no use to you,' he sneered. Perhaps it is good for the human spirit when totally and hopelessly deflated, to be roused by shock treatment. I reacted spontaneously.

'How would you like to be castrated?'

He was distinctly ruffled. 'That is not at all the same thing,' he blustered.

I looked into his inhuman rat's eyes. 'For me it is,' I told him, 'exactly the same thing. Without thought you are proposing that I be deprived of my most important sexual organ: the source of my womanhood. It *is* castration, and I refuse.' From the middle of the dark tunnel in which I found myself, I was yet able to note that he was disconcerted. He walked to his desk and started writing. I rose from the couch, arranged my clothing and sat down at his side. Ever since the blow had fallen I had been troubled by the fact that a latent instinct refused to be quelled. Although I felt ashamed of such a foolish feeling, I had to get an answer. Uncertain how to phrase my query, I asked timidly: 'Could this have anything to do with sexual intercourse?'

He dropped his pen as though electrocuted and turned incredulously towards me. In unbelieving tones he asked: 'Have you had sexual intercourse?'

I replied steadily, while loathing him: 'Over a very considerable period.'

He picked up his pen and turned it in his fingers for what seemed an unconscionable time.

At length he answered. 'It is just possible, but very unlikely.'

He started writing again. When next he looked up, he said he would make a reservation in a nursing home the next day, for the removal of the fibroids he had diagnosed with such speedy certainty.

'And what,' I asked, 'am I to do meantime? The bleeding is beyond any control. How am I to cope?'

'I can give you some pills,' he said tonelessly.

'Are they likely to have any effect?' I asked.

'No,' he replied.

In retrospect I wish I had turned on him. Who was he to treat another human being with such heartless, such brutal abandon? It would probably have been a waste of what reserves of strength and sanity I had left.

His carelessness gave his fellow surgeon a lot of trouble. By 10.30 that evening my GP was so concerned about the unceasing flow of blood that I was losing, that he called an ambulance and I was borne away to the nursing home, where I was received by the second surgeon in his dressing gown, he having been roused from his bed under the apprehension that I might need to be operated upon immediately. After examining the patient, he decided that drastic action could be postponed till nine o'clock the following morning. It would have saved me a further series of harrowing experiences had he done the job there and then, in justification of having left his bed.

He left me to the distinctly ironic realisation that I had landed up in a nunnery and, further, that some nuns are convinced that adulteresses are *not* their sisters under the skin; that Mary Magdalene got off too lightly and that it was up to the brides of Christ not to withhold the scourge to subsequent sinners. The night sister's manner was that of a wardress. She put before me the form that I had to sign giving the surgeon permission to remove any portion of my anatomy that he saw fit. I was now in a state of phobia regarding the fate of my womb. I was most reluctant to append my signature to the form, but, in the face of the contemptuous enmity of the wardress, I did. She had the godless gift of inducing utter humiliation.

She also put before me a letter. It was from my GP to the surgeon who was to carry out the operation. It expressed the opinion that Miss Wyndham's condition was due entirely to menopausal symptoms. It added, as an unlikely afterthought, that there was the faintest possibility to be considered that an incomplete abortion might be responsible for the massive and continuing haemorrhage.

The word 'abortion' sprang off the page at me. So that still small voice, that had whispered throughout in my intuition, had been right. I had conceived. But ABORTION! What a terrible word. They, the faceless medical authorities, who were causing me such unnecessary suffering; while unwilling to believe that I could have been pregnant, were quixotically determined that I was intent on destroying my own longed-for child. I rang for the virgin wardress. There had been a horrible mistake, I blurted out. I was not having an abortion. The wardress was distantly repressive. If I had got myself into this sinful trouble, it was assuredly not her business to listen to the results. If I had any problems I could name them to the day staff. Nothing more was due to me that night.

In the morning a nun bustled in to give me the pre-operation injection. I had begged the day sister that I might be allowed to see the surgeon before the operation. Only one obsessive thought filled my appalled mind. I had to make it clear that I was miscarrying, *not* aborting. I could not bear the thought that anybody, particularly the person in charge, should continue to have any illusions on that score. The sister said repressively that what I asked was impossible. It was the rule that no person saw the surgeon prior to an operation. She left the room.

By the time that she returned the injection was beginning to take effect. I pleaded with her anew. Whatever the rules, I *had* to see the surgeon. There was something terrible that had to be resolved without delay. She told me sternly to stop being difficult and to lie still. I raised myself in the bed and put my feet on the ground. I knew that I could not stand, but while the sister bustled round from the other side of the bed, insisting angrily that I lie down and be quiet, I took a tight hold of the end of the bed. As she tried to prise my fingers apart, I made a last desperate bid for understanding.

'Fetch the matron. You ought to know that what you are inflicting on me is very bad for me, drugged as I am. Whatever may happen will be entirely your fault. Fetch the matron.'

She rushed from the room. I stayed, clinging to the bedpost, waiting for yet another avenging angel. A large, elderly nun came through the door and said, in the kindest of tones: 'My dear, what is the matter?'

I blurted out a confused account of my agony of mind and how I must be allowed to see the surgeon. She said: 'You shall see him, my dear. And now let me help you back to bed.'

The surgeon came to my bedside, full of compassionate concern. He explained, what I still think is iniquitous, that in medical parlance only one word exists for the act of losing a foetus, and that word is abortion.

My first words on recovering consciousness were to ask had I got my womb still? I had. The relief was overwhelming. The future still held hope. 'There was a great deal there,' the surgeon informed me.

To be so overwhelmed by a crescendo of events that you have to struggle desperately to keep your head figuratively above water is, at times, a lifebuoy in itself. To come to terms with each successive minute demands so much determination and endurance that the psychological pain has no breathing space in the crisis. If Henry had gone through the ordeal with me, it would probably have been harder for both of us. An aborting woman is not a desirable object, and already his loyalties were sufficiently split. The following day, Pamela, hearing on the invariable rural grapevine where I was, came in her car and took me home to Petworth House, where I stayed two nights before resuming normal life. I was on my own again.

For the next twelve months we tried, in the intervals available to us, to arrange that I conceive again. Henry would make a special journey at any moment that I felt was particularly ripe for fecundity. Nothing happened. While I lived in a perpetual state of expectancy, I was not shattered when my hopes were unfulfilled. I realised that it would be an act of selfishness. Born into such unordered circumstances our child must have lacked a sense of security, of belonging to an established family unit. Possibly of even being wanted if things became more difficult.

Genetically he or she would be burdened by a double load of distrust. My fears of the worst were apt to be stronger than my hopes for the best. Henry compared his life with that of a juggler striving to keep several balls in the air at the same time and fearing that any one might slip through his fingers. If I could have had a son like *Jackanapes*, the hero of Juliana Horatia Ewing's intensely moving story! He had been brought up by a lone woman, to die a hero's death. I remarked what a good name 'Lollo' was for a horse: 'but you won't have heard of *Jackanapes*.' 'Of course I have heard of jackanapes,' he told me, 'only I thought that it was something to eat. I am sure that I have ordered "two jackanapes, please" '.

I wanted the baby to be Katina. A girl would be more fun to dress and, I hoped, easier to understand. To this day I have in my mind's eye the boy that I now feel my child would have been. I have seen him in all the stages of his growth. How many other women, I wonder, have experienced this fantasy?

18

ALLOCATION OF SHARES

At least the year in which we attempted to procreate another child bound us closer together and fostered the strong human instinct for discovery: mutual discovery of our basic characters and personal needs. I think it is an advantage for a woman not to be too overtly attractive. To have the need to take trouble over relationships and, of necessity, to explore the character of the other person and, in doing so, make herself of interest to him.

Henry still did not read a book unless I asked him to. He then confounded my conviction that he would, at best, skip through the first chapter, or possibly the last, by being able to give an informed opinion concerning its total contents. Somerset Maugham's account of the release of sexual repression in middle-aged woman, as described in his short story: 'Winter Cruise', fascinated him. He read it, at great speed, in bed one morning. His comments left me with the impression that neither he nor Somerset Maugham knew much about women. The thought that, at this late stage in his life, I was in a position to open up wide vistas of enlightenment enchanted me.

In the event I believe that he taught me more than ever I

166

taught him, other than that he could trust me. I do not think that he had trusted a woman further than he could see her since Marylee. I am in favour of the jealous male. Nobody is jealous of what he does not want, which is reassuring. And, operated with discretion, it can be a useful handle.

Henry had introduced me to his youngest brother, Joseph, and his superficially charming wife. This devout, if innocently hypocritical couple was intensely involved in forgetting that, as Joseph had been married before, to a women who was inconveniently still living, they were, in the eyes of God, living in sin. This blotting-out technique precluded entertaining a suspicion that anybody else might be doing just that. The dinners we shared with them, where the conversation sparkled, called for a censoring mechanism not to let slip any rash admission of a more intimate knowledge of their brother than the chance proximity of being country neighbours would entail.

After one such occasion I was sitting at the dressing table in our hotel room, brushing my hair, while reflecting on the satisfaction of time well-spent in good company. Momentarily I was less than fully conscious of Henry's presence, until he broke the silence and spoke. I turned in his direction. He was standing in the middle of the room in his shirt, his head bent despondently. What he was saying was spoken more to himself than to me. 'I don't know what to do,' were the words that had made me turn towards him. 'I am grumpy when I am away from you and I am grumpy when I am with you . . .' I rose and crossed the room and kissed him. What on earth was wrong to make him introduce this cloud into our own little clear blue sky?

In bed he nuzzled his face into my neck, as he always did when confessing to something of which he was ashamed. In a muffled tone of desperation I heard him ask: 'Is there *no* way we can get married?'

'No, of course there isn't. We are nice people,' I replied with all the mindless convention of a nanny placating a fretful child.

How smug I was. The plea was so at variance with what I knew to be his code of conduct that any caring, intuitive woman would have caught the note of lonely despair and talked the mood through with him.

Why does God, cry the fretful, let such dreadful things happen? Never do they ask why individuals, of their own free will, invite the states of human relationship that they later find they cannot bear.

The next morning, after breakfast in bed, I, still the practical one, suggested the comparatively prosaic plan that we should have another go at togetherness in the South of France, to make up for what had been bungled the last time. Henry said that he would do what he could to achieve this aim. To avoid madness it was necessary to believe him. Intuition warned me not to put great store upon any such actuality.

Why should I call it intuition? I had a working knowledge of the facts of his home conditions by then. What gifts I presented to Henry were naturally, and fortunately for the secrecy of our relationship, presumed to have been bought by himself. Any money he spent on himself struck at his wife's love-deprived heart and he was expected to spend an equal amount of money on her. I should have been able to deduce that when he returned from the French jaunt within five days, with the excuse that he had been bored, she would be unlikely to meekly submit to the expenditure of a further considerable sum with the object of boring himself all over again.

Of course this was not the explanation vouchsafed me a day or two later. That was trite in the extreme.

'Look here; don't you think it would be much better not going abroad? It is going to be very difficult. We may be found out. I think it is better to save our money for trips in this country. I've got several journeys coming up on which you could accompany me.'

Ah yes, indeed. The Newmarket run, where his time was fully occupied with every detail of the races or the sales; in confabulations with stud managers and trainers; while I walked for miles across the famous Heath with my dog, foolishly fretting at a less than perfect relationship that involved uncertainty, no sustained peace and security and, above all, the frustrations of what the French call *l'esprit de l'escalier*: the answer in a spirited discussion which always occurred to me after his departure, engendering an extra sense of loss, of the lack of oneness in mutual belonging.

The heart-sick human being who had sought reassurance for the doubt of the possibility of a total commitment, had now become this remote manipulator. That complacent woman who had pointed out that people as humane-minded as ourselves did not behave like that, now drew her man's handkerchief out of his pocket and mopped her embarrassingly streaming eyes as, striving to keep the irritatingly plaintive note out of her voice, she told him how much she longed for a reprieve from the brief visit.

He looked both hunted and mutinous. 'Well, what can I do about it? I come and see you every day.'

'You can't do anything about it. I expect it is stupid to remind you that when you said "Is there no way we can get married?" and I said there wasn't: we were nice people, I thought how smug I sounded. Now it is you who are being smug.'

I thought that he might well deny having used those words, but he did not. He made no answer. After a moment he put his arm round me and kissed me very kindly. We sat together; two unhappy people powerless to comfort one another.

I did not let it go at that. Both of us found a curious backhanded pleasure in making good antagonistic points in controlled, almost flippant, argument; me for, he against, what was, in my consciousness, a beacon.

If we had been able to marry would our mutual passion have lasted? People say that it never does when unopposed. They may be right. We never knew a period when, as two buckets in a well, we were at the same level for long enough to get accustomed to the other's presence, let alone to develop a sense of unwanted irritation at small recurrent habits that were second nature to the one who practised them. In all our years of stolen meetings we never lost the stirring pleasure evoked from the sensually satisfying embrace of our entwined bodies, skin to skin. Where this capability exists it is an invaluable ace-up-the-sleeve. In circumstances, inevitable in a long relationship, where a couple are temporarily unable to sympathise on a cerebral level, there remains the physical side to promote a total unity. Those who boast that they have never had a cross word, have not expended the necessary trouble and imagination of getting to know each other nor, in that context, themselves.

During the year succeeding my miscarriage Henry had said: 'I want you to wear my ring: so that people will know that you belong to me.'

I went to Bond Street in search of this much-desired bauble. In the window of Yeo, a small jeweller's opposite the more opulent firm of Asprey, I saw a dear little turquoise-garnished ring. I gave Henry the most exact instructions on how to find the shop and he departed to buy the ring of my choice – and returned empty-handed. He had not been able to locate the premises in question. Incredulously I took him in tow and returned to Bond Street. There was the shop, Yeo, and there was the ring in the window. How could he possibly have missed it?

'But of course I didn't see it,' he informed me, as one who states the obvious. 'Look, just next door is this art shop, with that picture of a naked woman in the window. I spent a long time looking at her. From then on I couldn't see anything else.'

The turquoise ring did not last long. It slipped off my finger while I was cleaning out the goat pens and fell into the manure heap, where it disappeared completely. The second ring, bought at a jeweller's in Newmarket, was an enchanting design of garnets and pearls. I still regret it deeply. I regard a ring as an emblem, not as a piece of jewelry to be put on and taken off to suit the mood or mode of the moment. Placed upon my finger, that is where a ring remains. Unfortunately pearls contract when immersed in water. After these had fallen out of their setting several times, I exchanged the ring for a single amethyst embedded in an intricate claw setting which would be proof against all eventualities. It was indeed a sturdy symbol of the hazards of our relationship.

Doubting, as ever, I wondered how long what I looked upon as the wooing period would last. To my surprise it persisted for three years, before the more useful whipping-post of his having someone to take pressures and irritations out on supervened.

It was not entirely a one-way street. I had gauged how important it was that I should be as much in the picture as possible regarding his relationship with his wife and the general scene at home. He was exceedingly reluctant to grant me any access to knowledge in this area. He gave himself away in certain aspects. When he accused me of habits and characteristics that were totally alien to me, I recognised that I was 'standing in' for his wife. If I questioned him about his wife, I was certain that he would fall into the trap of saying: 'leave my wife out of it.' I then sprung the trap by retorting: 'That is just what we will never do; and you should be ashamed of yourself for suggesting it. To leave her out of our picture is to betray her . . .'

I could then get the answer to almost any question I liked to ask. If he turned sulky I was ready with: 'Now you are treating me as you do your wife; but it won't do. Don't you ever go silent on *me*. You and I have always been direct with each other.'

It bred a climate of trust which ended in him relying on my judgement rather than his own. But it must have hurt. He knew how to hurt too. Driving back from London I said something about having half shares in him.

'Half shares?' he questioned, adding with deceptive mildness to hide, but not to blunt, the cutting edge. 'You have poking rights.'

An unsuspected hazard of accepting the role of Judy O'Grady (that name is known all over the world, an ex-Guards sergeant said to me) is that the colonel expects from her the same discipline he looks for in his men. Henry once remarked that he had considered the matter, and thought that he would be able to stand up to torture. I was surprised as he was almost as bad at bearing nervous tension as I am. However, when he joined the army, punishment on the wheel was still an accepted code of practice, and continued to be after World War I. He had been responsible for shooting a soldier who had gone absent without leave three times from France. The man had not been guilty of cowardice in the face of the enemy. His total concern was that his wife was being unfaithful to him. He could not prevent himself from making his way home to catch her at it. It was a predicament for which Henry must have sympathised. After two unheeded warnings the man faced the firing squad. It was Henry's duty to give the order to fire.

When I complained of the restrictive confinement of our situation, his reply was: 'If you love me you should show fortitude.' I was taken aback by the starkness of the statement. Thinking it over, I had to admit that it was an unarguable precept. Especially as it was followed by the presentation of a copy of the *New English Bible*. In this otherwise inferior version the word 'charity' in the Beatitudes has been changed to 'love'. There was a bookmark extruding from the page in question and the sentence, 'love keeps no score of wrongs', had been underlined.

How did he know about any of these things? He was the most unspiritual man I have ever met. But the one most able to keep on surprising me.

19

REGIMENTAL ORDERS

*T*here was the time when a neighbour and his wife invited me to accompany them on a motor tour from Rome, across the backbone of Italy, into Switzerland. Henry expressed himself as delighted, on my behalf, with the plan. He proceeded to paint the husband in the blackest colours, whenever the opportunity occurred. I realised that, in spite of his wife's presence, it was expected that he and I would seek and find opportunities for sexual intercourse. During the period before my departure on the Italian trip, I had every need to practise fortitude.

A few days before I was due to leave, Henry remarked that my dressing-table set — of sham tortoiseshell from the General Trading Company, that my mother had given me for Christmas many years before — was looking very scruffy, and he intended to replace it with a silver one from Mappin & Webb. I decided, in my own mind, that this was a pay-off present.

I packed it, as part of my luggage, and left on the night sleeper for Rome in utter despair. The next morning, speeding southwards, across northern Italy, in sunshine, I reached for my dressing case and unpacked the gleaming trophies. What the hell! I made myself think. They *are* beautiful. The door has not been shut. The situation may resolve itself. Meantime, take the opportunity to enjoy everything.

It was indeed a tour of fabulous interest and beauty: Rome, Caprarola, Gubbio, Perugia, Urbino, Florence. The town of interest that I can remember nothing of as a place, barring where we spent the night, is Viterbo. The hotel was situated in a narrow, uphill, alley. We had to wait behind a sports car, from the back of which a young man was unloading baggage in front of the hotel entrance. There was about his actions and general mien an ill-suppressed irritation. Standing on the pavement on the far side of the entrance, very much by herself and as if she had nothing to do with the car and the young man, was a girl. She was dark-haired and moderately attractive. What drew my attention to her was the air of pitiful embarrassment she bore. I identified with her instantly. She and the man were not married, and it was not working out for them.

When we, in turn, approached the reception desk, the young couple had just completed booking in. The man seized the bags and made for the staircase without a backward glance. The girl miserably followed him at a distance. Their passports still lay on the desk. I turned them towards me. They bore different surnames. I hoped desperately to see the couple at breakfast to judge if they had resolved their separateness. But they are imprinted on my memory to the exclusion of every thing of interest that Viterbo contains, from that one sighting only.

Our last night on Italian soil was spent near the Swiss border, at an hotel facing Lake Maggiore and the island of Isiobella, which we visited. I can remember nothing of the celebrated gardens there, but for a different reason. At the hotel a love letter awaited me from Henry, telling me how keenly he looked forward to my return.

Saved by the bell! as he, not infrequently, commented.

Occasionally Judy O'Grady scored a point. I was wont to accompany him, on the first Sunday in May, to the Cavalry Parade in Hyde Park. The old cavalrymen, in bowler hats, pin-striped suits and furled umbrellas, march, behind a band, past some poten-tate who takes the salute. There is a great get-together between officers and other ranks, recalling past occasions. I stood in the background, enjoying the absurdly nostalgic scene enormously.

One year in particular, I recollect. There was a regimental lunch at the Dorchester to conclude the proceedings, to which Henry, to my surprise, took me. We walked across the grass to Park Lane with two or three other ex-officers to whom I had not been introduced. While chatting to them, Henry unpinned his medals that he considered it in bad taste to wear off parade. 'Put these in your handbag, so that they'll be safe,' he ordered Judy O'Grady. His comrades kept theirs in place, having no camp followers in attendance. The medals were unexpectedly weighty. I quite saw that, in a pocket, they would spoil the line of a good suit.

At the Dorchester I was equally out of things at first, since I knew nobody and Henry knew them all. This state of affairs changed abruptly when the party went into lunch, which was presided over by the colonel commanding the regiment. I had known this officer when we were both young and had thought him rather a bounder. He greeted me as if we were old friends, which we never were, and placed me on his left side at the table. On his right hand was the elderly and dignified wife of the Colonel of the Regiment, who, perplexingly for the non-military minded, is not the same man as the colonel commanding the regiment. My acquaintance, to a great extent, ignored this august lady and devoted himself to exchanging a lot of jolly jokes with me, in which he included, now and then, most of the rest of the table.

I happily played to the gallery. I was not unaware that the colonel and I were behaving badly and that Henry was, rightly, disapproving. He left the table as soon as the meal was over, leaving me to follow him. We drove home in silence. Both of us were mulling over the likely implication that the bounder had recognised Judy O'Grady as such and had enjoyed jazzing up a somewhat stolid event at the expense of a former commanding officer. Henry was not in a position to reprimand me. I had simply obeyed regimental orders.

We did eventually go again to Cannes, more than once, because I thirsted so desperately for a few days' freedom from uncertainty and, always, the anticipation of plans that came to nothing or were interrupted. If life has taught me anything it is one should not be hot for certainties: acceptance is ultimately the only path to peace of mind. Ignoring my perceived fate, I met with yet more dusty answers in my heated search for certainties.

Henry had discovered the presence of a more sympathetic friend than M. Poignard in an old soldier called Guy Horne, who resided at Chateauneuf, near Grasse. We drove, in our hired car, to lunch with him.

'I quite see why Guy chose to settle here,' observed Henry in transit, 'the countryside is indistinguishable from Aldershot.'

Guy Horne was a kindly, benevolent person, who made us very welcome. He had thought to make living in France easier for himself by marrying a Frenchwoman. Neither side had been able to accommodate their way of life to the other, and they had ceased to live in the same house, though they still kept in touch. Her name was Hortense. One of the shocks in store for her may have been that Major Horne was uncompromisingly determined not to pay any lip service to the French language. He pronounced Hortense as if it was an English name. And it happens to be a French word that does not anglicise at all well.

We were, of course, also in touch with the Golf Club. One day I suffered from food poisoning and kept to my bed, feeling very ill. Henry insisted on keeping me company. About 7.45 in the evening he expressed his intention of going out to get a bite to eat. He would be back within the hour. At 11 pm he had not returned.

What does one do, deserted in a French hotel, with a man's luggage as well as one's own? It would not, presumably, be impossible to settle the account oneself and depart for Nice airport, alone? Should one remove all evidence of one's companion's identity, in order to avert an outcry on both sides of the Channel? No. His name and address was recorded in the hotel register. Did one slink home, and say and know nothing? Or report this momentous disappearance?

These thoughts had been passing through my head for the last hour. By 11 o'clock I could bear the situation no longer. I felt I had to share it with someone and get an objective view.

I rang Yvonne Poignard. I explained the problem in as few words as possible and waited for some sympathetic feminine support. Yvonne laughed. Her hilarity came in peal after peal over the line.

At this moment Henry came in and I slammed down the receiver. I pointed out that I had thought that he was dead and that Yvonne was a sadistic monster. He was properly contrite

I said: 'Nothing matters now that you are here. But where have you been?'

It appeared that, after having the bite to eat, he had passed the casino on his way back and had yielded to the temptation to go in, just for ten minutes. Within the precincts he had fallen in, unexpectedly, with another old comrade. From then on, time had been forgotten.

This sort of problem I could cope with. There was another type of stress that, increasingly, became too much for both of us. Despite my tactics, there remained an uncomfortable fear-ridden, unexplained area surrounding his home life that, even after Henry's death, remains, not buried with his ashes, but hauntingly miasmic with unresolved mystery.

On all the occasions when I explored abroad without him I, who had no orthodox religious faith, would light a candle in some superb Popish church and make a silent wish: Please may Henry stop supposing that I want to marry him.

If there was no church whose interior beckoned to me, I threw coins into fountains, with the same wish. It was the only thing that I could do. Quiescence has never come easily to me, since the exercise of it got me nowhere in my youth. Not to know; to have all one's puzzled enquiries and refutations swept on one side under the heading of banging on about things, became, by degrees, past endurance. He was the one who cracked.

20

THE REWARD OF
PATIENCE

*D*uring the first months of 1967 Joan got married. It was plain that she had acted as an invaluable buffer between her mother and stepfather, who would now have to confront each other as emotional strangers. I suspect that Mrs Halton had been aware of her plight and had been instrumental in persuading Joan to remain at home prior to marriage.

I said to Henry: 'Your wife will need you more with Joan gone. I will be ready to see less of you.' He was unable to understand this quaint point of view and assured me that Joan's departure from the nest would make no difference. It would appear to have come as a complete shock to him to discover that, without Joan's presence, the entire home atmosphere had altered. I also suspect that the realisation that I, an outsider, had foreseen a situation that had taken him utterly by surprise, was even more unacceptable than facing up to the emptiness of his marriage relationship. He became more difficult than I had ever known him hitherto. Fortitude was no longer enough. Attempts to get to the root of his moods were a fatal mistake. Yet the break, when it came, took me by surprise.

Henry rose from the sofa, where we had been sitting and,

with his back turned to me, which was significant, he launched into a furious diatribe of hate. I cannot remember one single word of what he said. I would guess that he was not wholly conscious of what words he was using himself. Anyway the words were not truly important. What mattered was the pent-up release of fury that was giving way like the waters of a broken dam. I stood, helpless, behind him, as one who watches, breathless, a seething cauldron of waters out of control.

When at length he stopped, he wheeled round and faced me.

'Now,' he said, 'you tell me what you think of *me*.'

The waters had poured themselves into an eddying whirlpool, with a deceptive stillness at their centre. I had no wish to be sucked in.

'You know what I think of you,' I told him. 'That you are a brave old soldier, who has never had much lasting care and attention, and I have been lucky enough to be able to give them to you.'

I was conscious that I was taking a mean advantage, and also that it did not matter what I said. There was no hope of getting through.

He left the room. He left the house. His car drove away.

I went to Pamela. I told her that what I wanted Henry to realise was that, as for some reason, he wished to leave me, I would never seek to hold his allegiance. But the indisputable fact remained that we had had eight years of total trust and understanding, to say nothing of the deepest love; so why could he not consent to take my hand, agree that both of us had much to look back on with pleasure, and part in mutual amity?

Pamela thought it a very reasonable suggestion and kindly offered to find an opportunity to put the proposition to him. By chance it happened within two days, when she saw him and asked him to come over for a drink the next day.

He came. As soon as my name was mentioned he put his head in his hands and burst into tears. Pamela was deeply moved. She was not accustomed to such unrestrained emotion in men. My brother, while not unknown to get into a rage, always remained dry eyed. Henry was obviously still in a great state of turmoil, whether facing me or my sister-in-law. He said brokenly, through his fingers, that I had made him happier than anybody . . . until I began asking questions. There had never been a time when I did not, and there never will be a time when I shall not, ask questions. He knew that. Something had happened that he did not dare answer. He agreed to come and say goodbye with good feeling instead of mindless fury.

One of the inexplicable elements that remains from this crisis and the one that resulted in his death, is why he should have agreed to carry out an act that he could not face up to.

When the government edict had gone out, requesting private citizens to hand in all but sporting firearms, Henry, with obvious reluctance, had surrendered his service revolver. I asked him why he minded parting with it? His reply profoundly startled me.

He announced, with toneless finality: 'Now there is no way out.'

A similar impasse appeared to have been reached. When he came into my sitting room, he sat down on the sofa, as rigid as a robot, staring straight ahead. He would not touch me or allow me to touch him, to hold his hand. So far from saying goodbye, he said nothing at all. He appeared to have decided that all that was required of him was his physical presence and that he had entirely honoured this commitment by appearing on my doorstep.

Helpless, hopeless, almost unable to believe what was happening, when he was about to take his departure, still without laying so much as a hand on my shoulder, I took his ring from my finger and formally handed it to him; thereby, thought I, relinquishing, by this gesture, all rights to him. Not even that worked. He placed the ring on the window sill and departed, closing the front door between us.

The Garden of Gethsemane should remain an eternal reminder to us that, in extremes, it is an act of unnacceptable presumption to expect sustained help from friends when in our greatest need. I rang up what I hoped was a reliable friend and begged her to come to me. About half an hour later, another friend, exhibiting every sign of reluctant embarrassment, drove up. The first friend had, by a simple telephone call, shifted the onus on to a less self-determined character.

The second woman, unknowingly and unwittingly, by not the slightest exertion on her part, was of use. Her obvious discomfiture and indecisiveness forced me to exert myself, to make decisions. Not for me the relief of collapsing in a jelly. *She* had already annexed the role of quivering.

We could not go on standing there, looking at each other, so I suggested that we went for a walk. I expected that she would want to know some details of my plight, to offer some advice or commiseration. Instead we slogged through the woods in silence. To be stunned is a merciful state. It is the coming round that is painful. It was that future feeling that I so greatly feared. I did not believe that Henry no longer loved me. I had no gut feeling that such was the case. On the other hand I had no useful evidence to the contrary. This state of contradiction totally bewildered me. I could not express it.

When we got home, since my friend had no guidance to offer, I cooked lunch for us both. While I did so she stood in the kitchen, looking miserable. As I busied myself preparing the meal, I was able to assess that it was in my interest to have something of immediate importance to do. I also felt, and felt increasingly, that I was the one with the prior claim to be miserable. In this sorry farce I was being upstaged!

After lunch my good friend spoke at last. She said that she thought that she ought to be getting back to her husband. I did not seek to detain her, but I stated that I could not possibly spend the long dark night alone. I must, whatever her views on the subject, spend the night in their house. She acquiesced. It was agreed that I should arrive at 8 o'clock and share their supper.

That left six nightmare hours to fill. I spent every spare hour of the day playing Patience. It calls for concentration. It excludes extraneous thought. I think I owe my sanity to playing Patience: I have never, and deliberately, played it since. Even if I was again faced with what I largely had to bring myself through on that occasion, the Patience would serve to remind me of teetering on

183

the precipice of despair, loneliness and the frightening incapacity to be allowed the remotest understanding as to why it was happening.

I made a nuisance of myself for a week by passing each evening and spending the night at the house of these friends, while playing interminable games of Patience during the day. It at once became plain that the husband found my woebegone presence a distinct and uncalled for strain. The wife continued to look sorrowfully at me, as if I was in some way deformed. This attitude roused me from my torpor sufficiently to draw her into my bedroom, when we all retired for the first night. There I subjected her to a torrent of tears and moans of 'How could he?' and 'Why did he?' solely in order to force some reaction. I failed. She only uttered one sentence. It was: 'I can't understand it,' and that was *my* line! But I think the outburst did me some slight good.

Within a month of these events my birthday came up. It was a date of which I had always had to remind Henry. This year, of all years, on the very day a parcel arrived containing a beautiful hall-marked silver powder compact. With it was a card bearing the highly unsuitable inscription: 'To wish you a happy birthday. H.'

I recognised that the sarcasm was unintentional, but the gift meant nothing to me in the absence of the vital word 'love' from the card. It would have been petty and causing a double hurt to return it to the sender. Equally, considering everything, I could not use it. I restored it to its wrappings and put it away on a shelf.

A further month went by with life proceeding somewhat like the flickering, out-of-focus colourlessness of an early movie. Sometimes, of an afternoon, I would go for a walk with the woman who had found herself pitch-forked into my disaster. When she was not forced to too close an inspection of other people's problems, she was a person of acute and knowledgeable intelligence, capable of focussing my mind on objective topics. One day we were walking along a country road when Henry, in his car, drove out of a side road, some way ahead of us. We were too far off for me to be certain that he had seen us. The fact that he had was manifested within the next couple of days.

It had been my pleasure to stand him the cost of a syndicate shoot in the neighbourhood. This was a great joy to me, as I knew how much he enjoyed shooting and I enjoyed hearing how the day had gone and of the people that he had met. Two days after that walk the money involved was returned to me in notes, with another curt message. This time it read: 'As I can no longer keep this, do with it what you will.'

Clearly he had supposed that the reason why he had received no response to the presentation of the silver powder compact must be because I was absent from home. I made haste to return the money to him, with the written information that as I had given it to him it was no longer mine to accept as such. I added that, having no idea why, under the present circumstances, he had sent me a birthday present, it was waiting, in its package, until I received an explanation as to what had prompted its despatch.

No further communication ensued until, with the approach of Christmas, my distress and continued bewilderment became harder than ever to endure. I wrote to him, at the Stud, not once, but I am afraid several times, letters marked 'Personal', begging, at this season of peace and goodwill, for a little enlightenment, an assurance that I would willingly and always abide by any decision concerning ourselves that he wished for. I got no reply.

Throughout that bleak midwinter of my soul I made it my business to discover what little I could of conditions pertaining within the Halton household. As far as I could ascertain nothing had changed. Henry still went on all his expeditions alone, his wife did not now play a greater part in his life than she had previously done. A blank space remained where I had been. I decided to leave things as they were until Easter, and then, unless conditions had meantime changed, make a raid.

One morning in April I found him in his office at the Stud. I was fortunate in that he was alone: his secretary was not there. He looked considerably taken aback at seeing me. I explained that I happened to be passing and proceeded to ask for news of various mares and horses in training. On this safe ground he responded spontaneously and, in no time at all, we had slipped, without noticing it, into the old easy intimacy.

When I said lightly: 'Come and see me one day,' the invisible wall materialised. He looked nervous and uncomfortable and began, without much conviction, to formulate excuses. I allowed myself to perch, for a moment, on the edge of his desk. I said: 'You can pretend all you want, but as soon as we began talking it has been as though we have never been apart — and you know it.' He capitulated, but not happily.

I cannot pretend that the resumption of our relationship was easy at first. Of course I wanted a few answers. I have never got them. And I still mind that. From the moment that I surrendered in the battle for information our intimacy resumed its strong mutual physical attraction and mentally became bonded by a greatly increased trust on his side, the sort of trust that he had only been accustomed to repose in a male comrade.

21
STEAK AND KIDNEY PIE

*F*rom thenceforth there was a general change of balance in our relationship. I found it possible and feasible to enter the Halton household. At a drinks party, a form of social intercourse I generally despise, Mrs Halton under the benificent influence of alcohol, became so affable that she actually said to me: 'You must come to lunch one day.' I accepted with alacrity. A week later I met her in Midhurst and, with nothing to lose, reminded her of this invitation. She did recall making it, but what was crystal clear was that the mood of the drinks party had worn off. I relentlessly persevered and she said, obviously with the intention of reneging on her careless words, that she would discuss the matter with her husband.

So did I. It was with him that the time and date were settled. It was a very curious experience. I arrived, as asked, at 1 pm. He let me in and, when his wife failed to put in an appearance, I asked where she was. He replied: 'In the kitchen,' from which no sound came. About ten minutes later I heard her coming down the stairs. She came into the room, looking as withdrawn as usual, and making no apology for her prolonged absence. At lunch I made it my business to ignore her husband completely and engage her in conversation on her one great interest: hunting. I was congratulating myself on how well I was succeeding when he, with equal success, proceeded to spike my guns.

Addressing himself exclusively to me and putting into his voice that modulation of implicit sex appeal that I had noted in his initial meetings with my female friends, he proceeded to remind me of experiences that we had shared, but as though I had not been connected with them. Several such instances had slipped my memory till that moment and the instinctive prompting to exclaim 'Oh *yes*, and *then* do you remember what happened?' was alarmingly difficult to suppress. I looked at Mrs Halton, but as we were not talking of hunting she had switched off. This was a relief. I recognised that it was indeed most unlikely that she had, or ever would have, any suspicion of her husband's conduct unconnected with her personal comforts.

It was the certainty that he was as ignorant of her perplexities that made me stay behind when he returned to his afternoon stint at the Stud. I helped with the washing up and performed some small menial tasks that Mrs Halton pointed out as being a wearisome burden. I condoled with her on the exhausting duty of having to prepare supper for two after a day spent following the hounds. She was gratified by my perspicacity on this point, but less than appreciative when I suggested that I should prepare a main course every Tuesday and leave it on her doorstep. It was not that such an act was asking too much of me, but that I was getting too close. When I reminded her of how onerous she felt this duty to be, it went against her nature to in any way lighten the picture she had drawn of how much she had to suffer. So I carried the day. Instinctively I knew that it would not work, but as psychological research it was too good an opportunity to miss.

Later that afternoon, when Henry paid his customary visit, I asked him how he had dared to be so indiscreet. Funny it had certainly been: uniting two elements of surprising me that he always retained, but, on more than one occasion I had been within an ace of giving the game away. Not only that, I had been astonished at his total recall of our mutual experiences. He listened to me, but all I got in reply was a bland 'I like to make my guests feel at home.'

What had also been difficult was that I had already been in the Haltons' house more than once in her absence. I had therefore to restrain any comment on the absence or change of location of any fitment or piece of furniture, nor to have a knowledge of where the cutlery, plates, dishes were kept. On those occasions I brought my needlework with me. In my code one did not make love in the wife's home. In his code it was the cosiest place to do so.

It was on one of these visits that I saw a photograph of Mrs Halton with her twin daughters when they were children. I was struck by the pleasant, kindly light in her eyes, so at odds with the tartness and self-absorption of the woman she now was. In conjunction with her husband's sense of guilt, I recognised that here was a situation on which to sit in judgement would be very, very wrong.

An analysis of the self-destructive element of human nature when it has decided that life is unfair was unavoidable, after I had made three expeditions to the Haltons' doorstep with dishes of the steak and kidney pie variety. After the third Mrs Halton's husband informed me that she had told him to convey the news that she no longer wished for this service. Ignoring the chance of being lacerated, I did not hesitate to point out that the arrangement had been made exclusively between her and myself. That she could not have the plain decency and good manners to communicate her change of heart to me personally, after accepting three dishes, I found no less than insulting. Again to my surprise, instead of castigating me, he said quietly: 'I know. There is no excuse. I am very sorry about it.'

Our final visit to Cannes presented, once more an awareness of the vital missing piece in the jigsaw that I desperately sought, to complete the pattern of an understanding of their flawed marriage. So many hitches had occurred that I despaired of the venture. Yet here we were, in bed, at the Hotel Mediterranée. I could not help asking hopefully in this intimate atmosphere: 'Do you think that Mrs Halton had, perhaps a suspicion that I was accompanying you?'

He replied ominously: '*What* did you say?'

I had been speaking into his ear, so this stalling was absurd. I answered steadily: 'You heard what I said.'

He turned on me. His hands came out, the fingers clawed into a strangling grip; his voice uttering the vilest insults. This had happened on two previous occasions: once caused by jealousy, once owing to another misinterpretation of an allusion I had made to his wife. But never before had I felt the stark terror that I did now. I not only rolled out of range, I left the bed and made for the furthest wall. When I turned to face the bed, the menace had gone, but the fury was still there. I asked: 'Just what did you *think* I said?' But I got no answer. I crawled back into bed. He turned his back to me. Half an hour later I could still feel his tenseness as a tangible 'thing' between us.

I put two fingers on his arm and said: 'Just turn over and face me. Don't speak. We will feel better then.' He did as I asked and in five minutes was sound asleep. I do not think that I slept at all, but I kept my fingers on his arm.

In the morning he said: 'I apologise for last night, but please don't ask any questions.'

It was the first and last time that he apologised for anything. Surely a clever woman, a Portia, could have extracted the vital evidence, then, when his defences were down. I obeyed him. I have never ceased to regret it. Owing to our mutual cowardice, the denial of the blessed quality of sharing, his death, when it came eight years later, was one of despair.

Apart from that little interlude, we had a very good time. Later that morning Henry rang up Guy Horne. I heard Guy say: 'Have you got the child with you? Good. Then bring her with you to lunch.'

'Is he crazy?' I asked, to be told that the term was soldiers' slang for a personal woman.

At lunch we found Peter Churchill, the British Resistance leader on behalf of General de Gaulle. I ventured to ask him what percentage of the French had been members of the Resistance, he admitted that it was difficult to say, but that he would not put the number at above three per cent.

22

LARCENY AT SEA

*I*n the autumn of 1973 I received an invitation from friends in Boston to go and witness the celebrated Fall as experienced in New England. I had not the guts to fly, so I booked a passage, tourist class, on the QE2. It was a very peculiar experience. The voyage was supposed to take five days, but owing to the ship's well-known propensity for breaking down, we drifted a further twelve hours in the Atlantic Ocean, mocked at by gulls.

Most of the passengers were on board in order that they could boast to their friends that they had made a voyage aboard the QE2. They had no intention of landing in New York, but were looking forward to a further bout of dancing and streamer throwing, while wearing funny hats, on the homeward run. They made me feel totally isolated — and on a desert island at that. I longed to use the ship to shore telephone, or that Henry would feel impelled to make use of it.

Seeking comradeship I sneaked up the stairs to the first class quarters. They were divided from the tourist area only by a padlocked chain, stretched loosely across the companion way. Beyond the chain the comfort level was considerably higher. The culture level was not, merely different. The deck was carpeted and enclosed by glass. On it rested long chairs. On the chairs reclined middle-aged women, expensively dressed and glittering with gold and diamonds: from wrist to elbow, on their fingers, at their throats, in their ear-lobes. Their talk was exclusively and monotonously of their hairdressers and couturiers. Actually they did not talk: they shrieked at each other. I brought my needlework with me and extended myself comfortably, in order to enjoy the sunshine through wind-proof glass.

For meals I was placed at the dentist's table. The wise man only appeared at it once, the evening before we docked. He gave the impression of having recently removed all his own teeth, as he kept his mouth clenched in a thin line. The woman on my right had introduced herself by saying: 'My name is Mrs Syrus Q. Honk. What is yours?'

I found this approach somewhat overwhelming. Would it be transatlantic good manners to reply, in form: 'I am the Honourable Ursula Wyndham'?

Not if it sounded as silly as Mrs Honk's approach had. Apart from that it was contrary to all my training.

On my left sat a taciturn, not unintelligent youngish man. The rest of those gathered at the round table were faceless. Its roundness made it possible for me to work off my acute boredom by firing questions at each person in turn and endeavouring to involve them in general conversation. In no way did I feel that I had succeeded. I was therefore not a little astonished when, after the last supper, Mrs. Honk bade me farewell with the enthusiastic words: 'I have *so* enjoyed your conversation.'

Before receiving this nosegay I had admitted that I had spent perhaps half an hour of every day in the first class quarters of the ship. Mrs. Honk took this information calmly. My compatriots at the table were openly shocked and disapproving. In short, I had cheated and was little better than a thief: taking what I had not paid for. I was much impressed by this puritanical honesty.

The one bonus of that voyage was the most skilled, imaginative and entrancing puppet-show that I have ever seen. Its chief manipulator, a young man, told me that he operated from Southport, his native town. The unprivileged tourist class was only permitted to view one showing of this distinctive art form, which had been engaged for the daily pleasure of the first class passengers. A final performance, at midnight, was also granted to them. Undeterred by the disapproval I had encountered, I would very much like to have attended this performance. Only the difficulty of keeping awake in the society of my travelling companions until that witching hour, held me back.

My kind hostess had flown down to New York from Boston, to meet me at the dockside. She bore me away to Greenwich Village, where a friend of hers had lent her apartment to shelter us for the night. Greenwich Village turned out to be not the elegant quarter that I had supposed, but the avenue in which the apartment we sought was located was fringed with ginkho trees, my first introduction to them. I was so fascinated by their effect and the unique beauty of their leaves which were beginning to carpet the sidewalk, that I was, unlike my anxious friend, who had mislaid the front door key, quite happy at the idea of spending the night sitting on the doorstep. A great improvement on life aboard the QE2. Fortunately, around midnight, another inhabitant of the building returned home. A friend of my hostess's friend, she had been forewarned of our impending arrival, and let us in.

The next day, after visiting the Frick Museum, Central Park and the Steufel Glass Shop, we caught the train to Boston. A flight would have been less eventful. The train lurched from side to side so violently that I saw no chance of it staying on the rails. I dropped from my seat onto my knees, explaining to the man who sat opposite to me: 'When the train leaves the rails it is safest to lie on the floor.'

He replied: 'When the train leaves the rails, the ceiling may become the floor.'

I saw the point of this advice and rose once more to a sitting position. Surprisingly there was no disastrous accident after all.

In Boston I had some difficulty in detecting which was the floor and which was the ceiling. Nowhere is a free-thinking democrat from Old England less at home than in New England. Edith Wharton's mother appears to be alive and well and living on Beacon Hill. Bostonians, by and large, like to think as one. To a pattern. It is reflected in their furniture which is Chippendale or Regency. Boston bred several notable furniture makers in the eighteenth century, who used the convex and concave shell pattern to notable effect. All this furniture is in museums, and that, thinks modern Boston, is the proper place for it. Convention also insists that any area containing book shelves is a library, even if it is no more than four feet square.

I had read the history of the War of Independence prior to this excursion and found it fascinating. It was very useful too. The whole of Boston is a memorial to the event. On this subject there need be no fear of a deviation of views. I was eager to learn more; the Bostonians were most able and ready to teach. If I tended to reflect that, in 1776, there must have been two schools of thought, but that, by 1783, these had been moulded into one that still prevailed, I kept these meditations to myself. Here my floor was their ceiling. I am only conscious of making one cardinal error. Before my departure I tactlessly named the woman who, of all the charming and intelligent people I had met, I felt to be the most charming and the most intelligent. My host gave vent to an intellectual explosion. Now he had heard everything: my choice was not only not in the Social Register, she had married an 'Irish mick'. I did not recant. Still less did I reveal that her individuality was what appealed to me.

I had written to Henry nearly every day. In return I received, at regular intervals, scrappy replies telling me virtually nothing, save the valuable information that, as the date of his regimental dinner coincided with that of my return, our reunion could be an overnight affair. Before leaving New York I had called at the office of the French opposite number of the QE2, the *Ile de France*. The clerk had greeted me blandly with the words: 'We have many defectors from the QE2.'

I booked my homeward passage on the *France*. She was not nearly so handsome a ship as the QE2, but she had certain advantages. The food was markedly better and the passengers more congenial. That is the tourist class passengers. Proof that the French character is less intrinsically honest than the English was offered when I attempted to explore the first class quarters. The companion way was barred by an obstruction that a cat burglar would have found some difficulty in surmounting.

At my table was a cosmopolitan American named Paul Davis. He made himself very agreeable to me, while remaining very reserved about the precise nature of his profession. He worked in Nigeria. In what capacity I was unable to discover. He would be leaving the ship at Cherbourg, at the end of its voyage, and proceeding to Paris by train immediately, although the ship did not expect to dock till the middle of the night. He professed to have made no plans as to how the journey between the docks at Cherbourg and the railway station at Paris was to be organised in the small hours.

I discussed this matter with a French woman in a wheel chair, who appeared to be an accomplished world traveller. She had much meticulous advice to offer on the subject. I relayed this faithfully to my friend, Davis, who appeared to be grateful for the information. At the last supper a direct contradiction of Mrs. Honk's friendly farewell was staged by Paul Davis. Before the meal was over he rose silently and left the table hurriedly. He did not return. I felt certain that he would appear before I disembarked at Southampton, but he showed no signs of doing so. I obtained from the purser the number of Mr Davis's cabin; on the door of which I knocked. There was no reply.

I felt for Paul Davis nothing more than gratitude to one who had enlivened what would otherwise have been a tedious voyage, but his disappearance before the end of dinner had been mysterious and I hate mysteries. When I got home I rang the shipping offices in Southampton to ask for his address. I did this with a certain interest as to what their response would be. Shipboard romances are celebrated. It was likely that they got many such enquiries and I suspected that a policy of giving no information would be customary.

This was not so. A lot of trouble was taken to research my enquiry. Finally the regretful reply was given that, as Mr Davis had continued on board until the ship reached Cherbourg they had no documentation on him at Southampton. They supplied me with the address and telephone number of their office in Cherbourg. Although I did wish to know how Paul Davis had made out on his unbooked journey to Paris, my interest was not sufficiently strong to ring Cherbourg.

I met Henry in London and, to my enormous relief and joy, the chilliness of the letters received in The United States bore no resemblance to the warmth of his welcome and expressed pleasure at my reappearance. It was the last time that we slept together. As such it remains established in my memory as a night in which we slept little, unwilling to squander in oblivion the mutual need expressed, the peaceful, blissful sustenance we found, safe in each other's arms.

I had found the way to crack the fortitude lock. There is just so much that an individual woman can endure. After reaching a certain depth it becomes more and more difficult to struggle, weighed down with misunderstandings, to the surface. It was a timely warning he had given me that I must never give way to emotion. I learnt, the hard way, the futility of it.

Instead I found out, with a sense of surprise, that if I played it cool, I could gain remission. I would telephone him amd say steadily: 'Look! you are constantly asking too much of me. I have stood too much, too long.'

There would be an expected expostulation of Nonsense! He had not the time to listen. I must work my problems out for myself. He had a lot on his hands. Not to bother him. And so on and so forth. I would listen silently until the flow had stopped. I then came back calmly, coolly with: 'You are not a fool. You know in your heart that what I say is true. If it wasn't I would not be saying it.'

There would then be a moment's pause. His next words were: 'All right. I am coming over.'

Whatever he was doing he would interrupt.

Within a quarter of an hour he was on my doorstep. I would be waiting in the hall. As soon as the door closed behind him, I put my arms round him and said: 'Thank you for coming.'

He replied: 'You know you can trust me.' There would be no recriminations, no score of wrongs. We took it from there. It worked.

23

HIATUS

Three months after my return from America, at the end of
January, 1974, Henry telephoned me one evening after
dinner. I remember that I was washing my hair and answered the telephone, dripping gently on to every surface. So many
of my friends take pleasure in saying reproachfully, as though the
telephone is visual: 'You have disturbed me washing my hair. It
is all wet. I cannot talk to you now.' I refrain from saying: 'Why
not? as you already are.' Me, I just drip.

Henry said that he had rung to warn me that he was coming
down with 'flu. He had never, over fifteen years, telephoned from
home in his wife's presence, before. I felt a sense of relief and
release as I told him I would ring back in a week's time to know
how he was.

A week later he told me that he was over the worst, but
feeling weak and would love to see me. I went over. He did seem
rather piano, so I only stayed a quarter of an hour. He
accompanied me to my car. Putting his hands on my shoulders,
he kissed my cheek. It was no more than a salutation between old
friends, but it was interrupted by a scream of fury from Mrs
Halton. She was standing on the doorstep yelling at him that he

was crazy to have left the house. She sounded so enraged that I returned with him to the door to greet her and make my apologies for not having forcibly prevented him from venturing momentarily into a mild afternoon. February, in the south of England, can be, on occasions, unexpectedly mild.

Having spoken to her, I turned to him and told him that I would look in again in a day or two. Mrs Halton glowering, rasped that there was no occasion to, as they were going away. I said: 'What? When he is not yet strong enough to stand the open air?' Disconcerted, she looked commandingly at him; willing him to make an answer. Looking at her, not at me, he recited obediently that that was right, they were.

I drove away feeling depressed and angry. What truce there had been was over. I rang up to enquire some days later. Joan answered. The story had changed. I was told that Henry did not feel up to receiving visitors. At this, he took the receiver from her and said: 'Pay no attention. I would like to see you.'

It was not only an abortive, but a most upsetting visit. It was difficult to talk through the tremendous banging of pots and pans that Mrs Halton was making in the kitchen next door. Finally she came into the room and, taking no notice of me, approached him. I cannot now recollect what she said, because all I remember is the look of stark terror on his face as he confronted her. I have never seen fear expressed so nakedly by a man. The knowledge and realisation of it shocked me to the core. No man should be that frightened of anything . . . And of his own wife! No wife should consciously rule by tyranny of the kind I had witnessed.

I knew that now Henry was going to the Stud for an hour or two every morning. The next day I drove there. I put my head round the office door and asked him to step outside for a moment — out of range of the secretary. I told him that I had had no idea that my presence was so obnoxious to his wife; that I would not be in touch again. When he had fully recovered I would wait for him to get in touch with me. He said: 'That is very sweet of you,' as if I had done him a small favour. That was all.

When he did re-appear at my house he was not the same man who had telephoned with cheerful resignation while I was washing my hair. He was low-spirited, withdrawn, and complained of an undefined noise in his head which prevented him from sleeping. After half an hour's quiet chat, I would ask him whether he could still hear the noise in his head. He would fall silent, appear momentarily to be alert and listening; there would be a long, long pause. Then he would finally slump back and say yes, he thought it was there still, but not as distinct as it sometimes was. Its presence seemed, in some remote way, to be of importance to him.

I gauged one way and another that there was some block between him and his wife which was weighing heavily on his peace of mind. She was not a woman whom even her children, who were on very good terms with her, could talk things through with. For this reason I suggested breaking the ice barrier by telling her that he loved her. Clearly she doubted it. Yet he had always told me, with too much persistence, that he did. So much more important to tell her.

'She would think I was mad,' he said.

'Very well,' I said, 'if you can't tell her, I will. This deadlock must be broken somehow.'

He objected. I was steadfast. Finally he said: 'Very well. If you think it will do any good. I have implicit faith in your judgement.'

There have been certain areas in my life where the answers I have sought have been denied me by the closing of invisible doors. This was one of them.

I drove to their house every day between twelve and one, an hour when most housewives, expecting their husbands home for the midday meal, are unlikely to be absent. Always her car was either not in the garage or, occasionally, there was somebody else's car standing on the gravel. Never, in weeks, did I get an opportunity to face her alone.

In early November, still in the depth of gloom, he was to go into hospital for tests to be taken with a view to establishing, beyond doubt, whether a probable operation on his prostate gland was necessary. He arranged with his secretary, Miss Nesbit, that she should keep me regularly posted as to his condition. Miss

Nesbit who, I had long suspected, was in love with him too, was explicit as to her reaction to the order.

'I want you to know, Miss Wyndham,' she told me, 'I am only agreeing to this because the Colonel asked me to.'

I assured her that I fully understood her feelings and was most grateful for her cooperation. As she knew, Mrs Halton was a curious and rather unhappy woman. I had tried to be friends with her, but she seemed suspicious of my motives.

'Has she any cause to be?' enquired Miss Nesbit pointedly.

Here it became advisable, as alas, it sometimes is, to depart from the strict canon of the truth, at least as Miss Nesbit would view it. 'But none,' I assured her. 'The Colonel and I have been old friends and neighbours for years. But I know she often makes use of you to do for her things that she has got all the time in world to do for herself, if she would take the trouble.'

'It may surprise you to know,' replied Miss Nesbit, 'that in all the posts I have held it has fallen to my lot to be called upon to do almost as much for my employer's wife as I do for my employer.'

Henry had promised to ring me from the hospital in the morning to tell me the result of the tests. When, at 1.50, I had not received the call, I rang him. He answered at variance so that I guessed his wife must be present, although, at that hour, I had supposed she would be eating her lunch at home.

Ten minutes later the telephone rang and his furious voice ordered me not to ring him, ever. His wife had said when he answered the telephone: 'I suppose that will be Miss Wyndham.'

I explained that I had waited till nearly two o'clock, when I naturally felt that she would have gone home to lunch.

He replied: 'She was late. I repeat, don't ever do it again.'

I asked and was told that the operation was to take place. Communication ceased.

I thought the matter over. This was not the time for fortitude. I reached for the telephone again.

'Please,' I begged, 'don't let us quarrel at a time like this.'

His answer came in an agonised cry:

'Oh, my darling, my sweetheart.'

As Dorothy Parker has immortalised, the telephone is the cruellest instrument for the purveyance of emotion. I could not take any more, God help me.

'Goodbye! Goodbye!' I cried and replaced the receiver. I had no inkling that it was.

He sailed through the operation, with no problems, as Miss Nesbit informed me. It happened that Pamela was temporarily a patient in the same hospital. I was due to visit her and decided that I would look in on Henry for a moment before I left. Another invisible door closed as I was told that he had been taken home earlier that very day.

From then on I had to rely entirely on Miss Nesbit. She called at his home every day for orders and consultations on her way to his office. She was punctilious in reporting to me. He seemed unable to take an interest in anything. He began to run a slight temperature. The doctor could find nothing wrong, but, to be on the safe side had Henry re-admitted to hospital for further tests. They proved negative, but still the listlessness persisted. The doctor was confident that it was just a question of time. Everything was in order, there were no complications of any sort.

The weeks, a month, and more weeks went by.

I was under the impression that I was giving nothing of my feelings away to Miss Nesbit. I was genuinely surprised when she told me that she had taken it upon herself to say to the colonel: 'I think that you had better get in touch with Miss Wyndham. If you don't, I fear she may try and come over.'

'Oh. And what did he say?' I enquired.

A slight note of awe informed Miss Nesbit's voice. She stated: 'He said: "She won't. She has a code of honour." '

The monotonous reports continued. He still continued to show no interest in anything. The doctor said encouragingly to wait until the spring. The warmer weather will make all the difference. I had recognised, during the summer, that he had lost interest in life. What both Miss Nesbit and I were banking on was his iron constitution and physical strength. I did not, at that time, realise that the power to opt for death is given to a small minority of people. Even if I had been aware of this fact I would not have associated anything I knew of Henry with the possession of such a power. Instinctively I knew that I could give him back his wish to live. I recognised, with equal certainty, that there was no way that I could get to him.

Christmas came. A Christmas card inscribed merely 'from H.' was delivered through the post; one of a number, Miss Nesbit informed me, that he was occupying a portion of his empty days by inscribing and directing.

On Thursday, January 16th 1975 I was due to stay the night in London with a friend to see the film *Murder on the Orient Express*. On the Tuesday I was obsessed by a strong instinct not to go to London. The feeling was still as strong on Wednesday. I had no idea what caused it. Considering the matter I wondered whether it was a warning that my car would be involved in a nasty accident. Since I consider it useless to attempt to avoid one's fate, I started out on Thursday apprehensively, driving with more than usual care. I arrived safely having encountered no hazards on the way.

I was now faced with another obsession. Being so helpless, I endeavoured to keep my acute anxiety about Henry and being deprived of his voice and presence, well to the back of my mind. Against my conscious will, my whole self could think of nothing but him. He permeated my entire reason. I remember, as if it was yesterday, standing, that afternoon, at the junction of Conduit Street and Bond Street, unable for some minutes to proceed, because my mind and will refused to focus on anything beyond his personality and presence. That evening, at the cinema, I hardly saw the film enacted on the screen, still less was I aware of the story unfolding. I saw it again, three weeks later, and it was as though I was seeing it for the first time.

When I awoke the next morning, Friday, January 17th, to my great relief the obsession had left me. I drove peacefully back to Sussex.

On Saturday, January 18th, I awoke to an unprecedented feeling of peace and serenity, basking in it I glanced at the clock on my bedside table. The hands marked the hour of seven.

At midday Miss Nesbit telephoned. She did not beat about

the bush: 'Bad news, Miss Wyndham, I'm afraid. The Colonel died at seven o'clock this morning.'

On Tuesday, she told me, he had felt poorly and had stayed in bed. By Thursday pneumonia had developed and he had been taken to hospital in a state of coma.

Nobody has to believe me. I know that he is waiting for me on another plane. I would not call it Heaven. That term is too simplistic in the unfathomable mystery of the Universe.

Since his death I do not feel that I belong either in this world or the next, since the two dimensions divide us. It is not an unpleasant feeling. It engenders detachment.